Plate 1:
Sensoji Temple in Asakusa, Tokyo. This is one of the most popular tourist spots in Japan.

Plate 2:
Kaminarimon Gate leading to Sensoji.

Plate 3:
New Year's at Kanda Shrine, Tokyo. Thousands of people visit to wish for a good year ahead.

Plate 4:
The Cathedral of Santiago de Compostela, Spain.

Plate 5:
Pilgrims traveling the Camino de Santiago.

Plate 6:
People climbing the *fujizuka*, a miniature replica of Mount Fuji, at Onoterusaki Shrine in Tokyo on July 1.

Plate 7:
Daimonzaka Hill of the Kumano Kodo pilgrimage route, Wakayama Prefecture.

Plate 8:
Sangui, a holy place in Sefa-utaki, Okinawa Prefecture.

Plate 9:
Traditional Shikoku
pilgrimage wear.

Plate 10:
Shurijo Castle, Okinawa.

Plate 11:
A pair of *maneki-neko* cat figurines at Imado Shrine, Tokyo.

Plate 12:
People praying at Seimei Shrine, Kyoto.

Plate 13:
Christ's tomb in Shingo Village, Aomori Prefecture.

Plate 14:
Women performing the *nanyadoyara* dance around Christ's tomb at the Christ Festival.

Plate 15:
A Shinto altar set up for the Christ Festival.

Plate 16:
A Shinto ritual performed during the festival.

Plate 17:
The *Lucky Star* mikoshi displayed during an annual festival held in Kuki, Saitama Prefecture.

Plate 18:
The Sengan Mikoshi and the *Lucky Star* mikoshi at the shrine gate during the evening of the festival.

Pilgrimages

in the Secular Age:

From El Camino to Anime

JAPAN LIBRARY

Pilgrimages
in the Secular Age:
From El Camino to Anime

OKAMOTO Ryosuke

Translated by
IWABUCHI Deborah, ENDA Kazuko

Japan Publishing Industry Foundation for Culture

Note to the reader: Japanese and Chinese names are written family name first, as is customary in East Asia.

Pilgrimages in the Secular Age: From El Camino to Anime
Okamoto Ryosuke. Translated by Deborah Iwabuchi and Enda Kazuko.

Published by Japan Publishing Industry Foundation for Culture (JPIC)
3-12-3 Kanda-Jinbocho, Chiyoda-ku, Tokyo 101-0051, Japan

First English edition: March 2019

Originally published in Japanese under the title *Seichi junrei: Sekai isan kara anime no butai made* by CHUOKORON-SHINSHA, Inc., in 2015.

Jacket and cover design: Fukazawa Kohei
Book design and DTP: Guild, Ltd.
Photographs for pages 45, 46: Aflo

Printed in Japan.
ISBN 978-4-86658-064-7
http://www.jpic.or.jp/japanlibrary/

Contents

4-15-19 Gift Japan Lib Project

Author's Introduction to the English Edition

I am delighted that an English translation of this book has been brought out by Japan Library. The field of religion and tourism is a new one that only began to receive attention at the beginning of the twenty-first century. I hope that this work contributes to the field and broadens it by including data that is specific to Japan.

Studies on religion and tourism in this country were pioneered by my mentor, Professor Yamanaka Hiroshi of the University of Tsukuba , and I wrote this book as part of the vision he shared with me.

My main interest is in modern religion in a secularized society. The theory of secularization first became a part of Western religious studies in the 1960s. The theory then was that religion would lose meaning as society modernized.

By the early 2000s when I started my graduate study, however, researchers were beginning to pursue a post-secularization theory that discussed the various ways in which religion continues to exist in society. In short, focus shifted toward the transformation of religion, not its decline. This book follows the post-secularization theory by focusing on how religion has been transformed by being mixed together with tourism.

My initial research theme was Catholicism in France. I visited many churches there on Sundays, but found few traditional believers. I was afraid that the original secularization theory had been right and religion was doomed. Next, however, I went to the Notre-Dame Cathedral and the Chapel of Our Lady of the Miraculous Medal in Paris, both of which were teeming with tourists. There were even more sightseers in Lourdes, at the monastery of the Taizé Community, and in the pilgrimage destination of the Cathedral of Santiago de Compostela in Spain.

I came to realize that people were visiting these holy places not just as tourists, but to acquire experiences that were religious in nature. That is, I saw people on journeys—pilgrimages—that were neither purely religious nor purely secular. It was after this realization that I turned to the theme of religion as a form of tourism.

Although I began my research in the West, I came full circle back to Japan to discover that the same situation was playing out in my home country in the mainstream Japanese religions of Buddhism and Shinto-ism, as well as other ancient faiths. I have included information on many pilgrimage destinations in Japan, and I will be pleased if the discussions here are referenced not only for religious and tourism research, but also for studies of Japanese and East Asian culture.

I wish to express my sincere gratitude to the translators of this book, Deborah Iwabuchi and Enda Kazuko, as well as editor Cathy Layne, cov-er designer Fukazawa Kohei, and team coordinator Urata Mio.

Foreword

What sort of place comes to mind when you hear the words "sacred site" and "pilgrimage"? We in Japan may think of Shinto shrines and events, such as Izumo Grand Shrine, one of the most ancient Shinto shrines in the country, or perhaps the Shikinen Sengu ceremony that takes place to mark the rebuilding of the Ise Shrines every twenty years. Then there are the sacred Buddhist sites on Mount Hiei and Mount Koya. Nearly everyone in Japan visits shrines and temples to pray for the New Year; some of the most auspicious places are Meiji Shrine and Sensoji Temple (Plates 1 and 2) in Tokyo, and the temple of Shinsoji at Narita.

Mountains have also been objects of veneration in Japan since ancient times. One is Mount Fuji, which was recently named as a World Heritage site; other important sites are the mountains Tateyama and Hakusan, and the Three Mountains of Dewa (Haguro, Yudono, and Gassan) in Yamagata Prefecture.

Outside Japan, Jerusalem and Rome are holy sites for Christianity, Mecca for Islam, Benares and the Ganges River for Hinduism, and Uluru (Ayers Rock) for the Aborigines in Australia, to name just a few.

Next, let's consider who you might find at any of these sacred places. Visitors to Kyoto and Nara wouldn't think of making the trip without stopping at shrines and temples there. Tourists in Paris will certainly stop in at the cathedrals of Notre Dame and Sacré-Coeur regardless of whether they are practicing Catholics. That's right: sacred sites are places for both tourists and the faithful.

I imagine that many people go to these holy places expecting to have contact with the core of the culture of the area. These sites are receptacles of historical memory, they express the values and world of the people living near them, and are often at the center of local identity.

In human society that is constantly in flux, sacred sites are important symbols, handed down through the ages, seemingly unchanged. But it should be noted that even ancient sites do indeed change along with the times. Sites that have been neglected may suddenly be brought back to the fore or connected with another spot, or even newly imagined. In this day and age especially, sacred places are seeing huge changes as they are linked to the familiar activity of tourism. It may seem strange to readers, but this book will consider these two issues—pilgrimages and tourism—together as a set.

When people think of pilgrimages, the image of a devout believer generally comes to mind, one who is motivated by a strong faith and who prays fervently. Although pilgrimage is a form of travel, we imagine going on a pilgrimage as quite different from traveling for pleasure. For the average Japanese, a religious pilgrimage probably feels far removed from everyday life.

It turns out, however, that the familiar act of tourism is an important key to examining modern pilgrimages. As mentioned above, holy places are full of tourists. Fewer and fewer people are fervent believers in any faith and there has been a decline in everyday occasions that have religion at their center.

What are the academic discussions on tourism and holy sites? They can mainly be summed up as having dismissed tourism. Tourists have always been seen as curiosity seekers who invade and tread on holy places. Academics devoted to the field of pilgrimage study have criticized tourists as frivolous.

But separating devout pilgrims from secular tourists is not so simple. Most Japanese do not visit temples or shrines other than to pray at the New Year, go to a wedding or funeral, or visit as part of a vacation trip. If you look at the homes of young people, few have ancestral Buddhist altars or traditional *kamidana* shelves for making offerings to Shinto gods. Not many people stand before these household holy spots in the morning and evening to offer a quick prayer.

However, one reason for going to a shrine, temple or church is tourism. What if someone turns on the television or opens a magazine and finds out that Hakone Shrine is a "power spot" for finding love? This person then spends the night at a Hakone hot spring and decides to stop by the shrine. Is this a religious pilgrimage or secular tourism? Is the visitor a pilgrim or a tourist?

The closer we look, the more it becomes clear that divisions of religious and secular, pilgrimage and tourism are no longer relevant. These days "praying tourists" and "pilgrims who come to play" are on the increase. One clear example in Japan is the spread of trips that combine visits to hot springs with visits to power-spot shrines—these are activities that are both secular and religious.

Contact with religion as a part of tourism is diversifying. It is possible to experience religion without belonging to a particular religious organization. In order to grasp this phenomenon, we need to focus on both "religious experiences for the religious" and "religious experiences for tourists." Accordingly, this book is not about the practices of a small group of fervent believers, but about situations that are familiar to most people. Our examination will include travel to UNESCO World Heritage sites; tourism that includes temples, shrines and churches; treks to power spots to find oneself and experience healing; the search for the mysterious and supernatural; the graves of famous people; and even settings for animation productions, Japan's renowned "anime."

We will look at people living in towns that are candidates for World Heritage designation, examining their pleasure and their confusion. We will also consider cases where citizens are attempting to establish a new tourist spot or holy spot in their locale, and listen to the voices of villagers seeking to lure in tourists with ancient traditions.

Each chapter in the book provides many case studies. The foundation for our discussion here is recent research on religion and tourism as a part of religious social studies. Some places have been revered as holy from ancient days, others have been rediscovered in recent years. We will also look at places considered holy because they have been used for the settings of fictional anime stories. Underlying them all is the same issue. How should holy places and objects be expressed and presented in the modern era when religion is no longer self-evident?

In the past, myths and the words of clergy were considered to be the truth. Things are not as clear-cut today. People no longer accept the entirety of religious teachings. This book will explore how sacred sites are established and how they survive as special places. We will also look at how changing attitudes to religion have brought about a basic change in modern-day pilgrimages.

Okamoto Ryosuke

The Background to Modern Religious Pilgrimages

Introduction

Religion does not have the influence it once did in Japan or the West. Fewer people are active members of organized religions, and communities no longer center around churches, temples, or shrines. How should we position religion these days, and what should our relationship be to it?

This chapter will take a look at the position of religion in modern society from the viewpoints of secularization and privatization, which have created a need for multifaceted perspectives on religious beliefs and practices.

The link between religion and tourism

In Japan's past, there was a connection between the activities of religion and tourism. For example, during the Edo era (1603–1868) there were four mass pilgrimages made to Ise in 1650, 1705, 1771, and 1830. These long trips, made in groups of several million of the faithful, most likely included elements of tourism, as described in the picaresque novel *Shank's Mare* by Jippensha Ikku, published in a series of installments between 1802 and 1822.

The Edo military government placed restrictions on travel by common folk, and trips for pleasure were not allowed. Thus the premise of a pilgrimage to the Ise Shrines, an important sacred spot in the country, was the perfect opportunity for most people to leave their daily lives behind and see the world. These journeys were known as *okagemairi*, or thanksgiving pilgrimages.

Classic *rakugo*, comic verbal storytelling, includes tales of travel motivated by both religious belief and the desire to sightsee. One rakugo tale is "Oyama Mairi" [Pilgrimage to Oyama], which is about making the trip to Mount Oyama's Afuri Shrine in Sagami, a sacred spot for Edo common folk. The story describes the commotion frequently caused by Edo natives, who were always brawling in taverns. We learn from the narrative how participants enjoyed the process of the trip and not just the actual visit to the shrine.

Back in the Edo era there was no differentiation between religious pilgrimages and secular tourism; they were both aspects of the same experience. But when Japan began modernizing in the Meiji era (1868–1912), visits to sacred spots came to be considered as separate from tourism. Pilgrimages were religious, and tourism secular. Pilgrims with religious beliefs made trips to achieve a religious experience. Tourists, for their part, purchased and consumed travel for their enjoyment.

This situation, however, is once again in flux. Religious and secular activities are no longer completely separate; they are connecting and changing. This book will focus on the sociocultural changes that have come about because of the fusion of religious pilgrimages and tourism. Long ago, the two were part and parcel of the same experience and now you could say they are blended. Our main objective here is to find the meaning behind the blending process.

What are pilgrimages?

How have religious pilgrimages changed from the days when they were integrated with travel for pleasure? Let's start by considering the meaning of the word *pilgrimage*. A simple definition might be "a journey to see where saints or originators of religions were born or buried, places that had a connection with those persons during their lives, or spots linked to gods and spirits." In other words, a holy or sacred place has a special status for a religion. Pilgrimages are religious practices.

In Japan, such journeys include the Shikoku Pilgrimage around eighty-eight temples on the island of Shikoku that are associated with Kukai, the founder of Shingon Buddhism. They also include climbing the sacred mountains throughout the country that are believed to be inhabited by deities and ancestral spirits. In the West, two of the most sacred Christian places are Bethlehem, where Christ was born, and Jerusalem, where he was crucified. Visiting them would fit in with the definition in the preceding paragraph.

From another perspective, however, this definition does not completely match modern practices. Let's go back to the reality of the decline of organized religion in most developed countries. Religion is having less and less influence on society. What, then, is behind the growing practice of pilgrimage? Devout believers of specific religions are not the only ones to visit sacred places. The simple definition set out above requires a connection to God or the Buddha or another supreme being to make a place sacred. In other words, there is a story that links the spot to a god, saint, or spirit that establishes it as special.

To someone without beliefs, tales about a place where a giant died in ancient times and the earth began, or where the ancestors of royalty descended from heaven must seem ridiculous. To nonbelievers, the story behind a sacred spot is a myth or legend, certainly not verifiable history.

You could say that accepting a myth or legend as truth is religious faith. Take, for instance, the fundamentalist Christians of the United States, many of whom believe that history happened exactly as described in the Bible. For example, they accept as truth the biblical story that the world was created several thousand years ago over the course of six days. For these types of believers, sacred places are a special part of their connection to a supreme being, and nothing will make them waver from their beliefs.

Still, does this mean that sacred places are only important to those with a fervent faith? Should these places be available only to passionate believers? Is it meaningless for others to go? Probably not. As mentioned earlier, in Japan and in the West, people visit sacred places whether or not they believe in their sanctity. Nowadays, visiting temples, shrines, and churches is an accepted part of tourism.

Tourists or pilgrims?

Since the beginning of the twenty-first century, increasing numbers of people have been following the Camino de Santiago, a pilgrimage route of several hundred kilometers to the shrine of Saint James the Great, in Santiago de Compostela in northwest Spain. This pilgrimage will be discussed further in chapter 2, but it should be noted here that despite a developed system of transportation, many visitors are choosing to walk the route. If the main goal is to visit a sacred place, there are few benefits to walking, which requires a great deal of time and money as well as taking a physical toll on the traveler.

The pilgrims, however, are not exerting all this effort in order to strengthen their faith. More than half of those walking to Santiago de Compostela are nonbelievers and many have never entered a place of worship of their own accord. It appears that the majority are not Christian. What we see here, therefore, is an increase in "nonreligious pilgrims." This situation is not limited to a town in Spain. The same trends can be seen in Japan with Shikoku pilgrims and visitors to so-called power spots.

Another example that shows the increasingly fuzzy line between pilgrims and tourists is the Roman Catholic Church's World Youth Day, an event that was first held in 1984, initiated by Pope John Paul II. Since then, the event has been held once every few years in a chosen city. Young people from all over the world gather at the location for a week of activities and exchange.

The influence of the Catholic Church on its youth has been in decline since the middle of the twentieth century. But recent World Youth Days have been attended by several hundred thousand to several million young people. Two-and-a-half million were at the event in Rome in the year 2000. Italian sociologist Luigi Tomasi states that it was impossible to divide participants into categories of tourists, believers, curiosity seekers, leisure guests, or pilgrims (Tomasi 2002). The important thing to remember here is that this difficulty in categorizing types of participant is the case in most modern-day pilgrimages.

Tourists without faith visit sacred spots and have a special experience. Some leave with new values or different ways of looking at the world. They appear to have a religious experience with no connection to any particular organized religion. From this perspective, we can see that our original definition of pilgrimage is inadequate. How do visitors who can be categorized as neither tourist nor faithful perceive the holiness said to be connected to sacred places? If visitors do not believe generally accepted religious explanations, why do they decide to make the trip?

Then there is the matter of new sacred spots and pilgrimage routes. Later in this book, we will look at places that have not traditionally been considered sacred, but are being promoted as such to bring in tourists and stimulate local economies. In Japan, even visits to locations used in films and anime are referred to these days as "pilgrimages."

Traditionally, pilgrimage sites were considered special places with a sacred aspect, visited by enthusiastic believers. This definition is no longer adequate. Indeed, it is time to admit that religion is no longer exclusively linked with churches or other religious organizations.

The secularization process

So, why do pilgrimages abound despite the decline in belief in gods, spirits, angels and saints, as well as demons? (At any rate, fewer people admit to taking their existence as an undeniable fact.) To understand, we need to examine the concept of secularization.

The society we live in has reached its present state through modernization, a process that also means a release from religion—in other words secularization. Society has been removed from a state in which the majority believe in a supreme being to one where the majority no longer do.

Let's compare modern society and its premodern counterpart. In the latter, religion had an enormous presence and influence. Most European nations declared Christianity their national religion. Monarchs maintained power with the backing and approval of the church. Education and medicine were administered through schools and institutions established by the church. Sunday services were not merely religious rituals, but an affirmation of one's membership in the community, of which the church was the center. Even today, travelers find churches at the centers of most European cities and towns, where the hours of the day are marked by church bells.

In Japan, during the early Edo era (1603–1868), a mandatory temple-membership system was established as a way to finance Buddhism and prevent the spread of Christianity that had been brought by foreign missionaries. This made Buddhism the de facto national religion and placed temples in charge of controlling local communities. By monitoring the population in this way, temples played the roles of both police and municipal government. This uniquely Japanese system continues today in a more relaxed form, with entire families enrolled as members of certain temples.

For people living in a premodern society ruled by religion, experience of the world around them was kept within a religious framework. In the Christian world, infant baptism was an affirmation of an individual's existence, and it officially welcomed them into the church community. There was a widespread belief that last rites administered by the clergy before death were mandatory to get into heaven. The church was at the center of community life and its influence was enormous. Even if legal systems were run by governments, laws were based on religious ethics and guidelines because there were no other sets of values or perspectives that could have replaced them. Religion was like a canopy over society.

Secularization is the process of loosening the grip of religion. British sociologist Bryan R. Wilson defines secularization as the process in which religious systems and consciousness decline as part of a rise in social consciousness (Wilson 1982). As we know from living in a secularized society, in many aspects of life we are required to think and act in a rational manner. When it comes to marriage and death and other milestones, religious ceremonies and procedures are no longer all that is needed. In this day and age, important stages in life must now be registered at city hall in order to be socially accepted.

The drive to behave in a rational manner can be seen in some of the smaller details of daily life. Here is another example presented by Wilson. Two cars arrive at an intersection. Let's say the car at the green light yields—out of an abundance of thoughtfulness—to the stopped car at the red light. Despite the warmth of feeling, this is a dangerous thing to do and would be inviting the stopped car to break a law. The situation does not call for religious virtue or ethics; it requires people to follow laws based on rationality. As we succumb to these rational measures, our daily lives are gradually cut off from religion.

The move away from the church

In the West, secularization is evident from the way people are leaving the church. In a 2006 public opinion poll conducted in France by survey agency CSA, only 8 percent of the Catholic population regularly attended Sunday mass, while 9 percent went once or twice a month. On top of that, most of the attendees were elderly. Estimates say fewer than 2 percent of people in their twenties go to mass. The same trends can be seen in Great Britain and other countries in northern Europe.

Churches outside of urban areas are being sold. Their high ceilings make them good spots for circus practice and carpet shops. As Christianity declines in the West, there has been a rise in the Muslim faith. Some churches have been turned into mosques. Or, church services are held in the daytime and rented out to Muslim communities for evening prayer.

Just because secularization is progressing, however, it doesn't mean religion will disappear completely. Many debates on secularization are taking place, about, for example, what it means in the West and in other regions, and how it affects religions with a single god compared to other types of religion (Nakano 2002). It is not easy to pinpoint when Shinto or Buddhism, religions without regular weekly services, began to feel the effects of secularization. In the course of this book, however, it should be borne in mind that in Japanese and Western societies, religion is not self-evident. The presence of a supreme being or the preaching of a particular religion in a public place are not taken for granted.

The spread of personal faiths and the impact of privatization

In premodern society when the presence of religion was taken for granted, people were not just physically part of a community, but also culturally and ethically. Take France, which used to have Roman Catholicism as its national church and had a population that was almost entirely Catholic. In those days, people must have had a general peace of mind, knowing that if they had any sort of ethical struggle or other problem, most other people would reach the same conclusion they did. The same held true for interpersonal relationships and everyday customs. Not everyone, of course, was deeply versed in Catholic teachings, but people were certainly raised according to the same customs and value systems.

A secularized society, on the other hand, does not have a dominant value system or culture. Except for a minimum number of rules and established laws, one can never be sure of the ethics and norms any particular person might adhere to. Acts such as murder rarely need be debated as to good or evil, but we can never know exactly how people stand when it comes to ethical and value-related issues such as euthanasia, abortion, same-sex marriage, organ transplants, or drug use. Going further, you could say that even if it was clear that murder had to be punishable by law, different people may consider the act as having varying degrees of evil. One can never be sure whether members of a secularized society share the same worldview. Common attitudes toward community and friendship as well as other shared values are breaking down.

With the progress of secularization, some religions are losing their public positions, resulting in diversified values and perspectives. This makes it more difficult for people to form connections other than physical, and means that religion no longer acts as a social compass and becomes further removed from public endeavors, such as politics and education. So, what position is left for religion? It becomes a private matter for individuals. This is what is referred to in this book as "privatization."

The privatization of religion describes two situations. One is a religion that, in a premodern age, was at the center of the public world and ruled the perspectives and values of society, but has now shifted into the private realm. As a result of secularization, the religion has been shifted from a social to an individualized position. The second situation is a lack of connection to a religion's original history or doctrine. It means individuals use only parts of the religion, or combine it with other religions. This results in customized beliefs.

Sociologist Thomas Luckmann calls this sort of belief an "invisible religion" (Luckmann 1967). He says that modern people do not accept the entirety of a religion's teachings or doctrine, but use only the parts that are convenient for them.

In premodern society, almost all people shared the values and perspectives of the dominant religion. Shared ethics and norms existed, and everyone tended to follow them. Luckmann states that in a secularized society where a specific religion is no longer shared, religion is used more as a point of reference, as a product that can be selected and purchased whenever it is useful.

Religious organizations want their believers to follow their entire doctrine. Believing only parts of that doctrine and mixing those parts with other beliefs is generally not allowed. To borrow a phrase from Luckmann, religious doctrine and ceremonies are offered as a "complete set." Breaking the set into pieces for individual consumption was never considered in the past. Nowadays, however, due to popular demand, religion is frequently sold by the piece.

One example of this is yoga, which originated as a traditional religious practice in India. Today it is offered in the form of classes for maintaining health and losing weight. There are some who study yoga and its doctrine, but it can be assumed that most modern-day practitioners fail to consider it a religion. Yoga has been misappropriated as spirituality.

The words *spiritual* and *spirituality* came into popular use in the mid-twentieth century as part of the New Age movement in the West. What is important here is to note that they are not strongly associated with existing churches or other organized religions. In other words, "spirituality" is, as a result of privatization, a word that can deal with a diverse range of privatized religions outside of the structure of traditional religions (Ito 2003).

Sacred grounds and stories

Today, pilgrimage to sacred spots is greatly influenced by privatization. Traditionally, pilgrimage destinations were controlled by religious systems and organizations. All holy places had a story that explained why the place was special. In Japan, for example, most shrines and temples have histories that tell how a certain god or Buddhist deity came to be enshrined or worshipped there. Traditionally, religious organizations decide what the story of a particular holy place should be, and then they can control these places and how they are used.

Mount Fuji, for example, has a story that connects it to the goddess Konohana-no-sakuya-hime-no-mikoto. For Sengen Shrine, the mountain itself is the object of worship. Another Japanese story relates to Kukai, the ancient founder of Shingon Buddhism. In an inner sanctuary of Mount Koya, the center of Shingon Buddhism, there is a mausoleum to worship

Kukai. Shingon holds that Kukai did not die, but fell into a deep meditation that he continues to this day in the mausoleum. Food continues to be offered to Kukai twice daily at 6:00 a.m. and 10:30 a.m. in a ceremony called *shojinku*.

The latter is a good example of how religious organizations have used myths and legends to control and maintain sacred places and keep them special. The meaning and location of a place depend on the authorized story of the organization. As privatization progresses however, a story perpetuated by a religious organization about a particular spot becomes just one of many stories. Individuals who are not members of an organized religion and have no traditional beliefs bring their own stories with them to sacred places.

The increase in the number of pilgrims on the Camino de Santiago pilgrimage route mentioned previously is certainly due to privatization. Those who travel the route do not necessarily believe in the story of Saint James as presented by the Catholic Church. In other words, the place has been separated from its traditional religious story. There is, however, among pilgrims, a desire to strengthen their soul and achieve self-actualization.

In Japan, another example of privatization is the "power-spot" phenomenon, which will be discussed fully in chapter 5. One such power spot is Hokkaido Shrine in Sapporo. It was founded during the Meiji era (1868–1912), as a political symbol of the defense of Japan's northern territories from Russia (Toishiba 2012). In its grounds are a number of other shrines, including the Pioneer Shrine that worships the people who first settled the wilderness of Hokkaido; the Sapporo Mining Spirit Shrine to comfort the souls of those who lost their lives in the mines; and Hotaki Shrine, the burial place for long-serving executives of the Hokkaido Takushoku Bank. All of these shrines reflect Hokkaido's history and sense of place.

Recently, Hokkaido Shrine has been appearing in the media as the greatest power spot on the island of Hokkaido. More and more people are visiting because they believe it will improve their chances of finding a love match or making money. There has also been an increase in tourists from Taiwan and Thailand. This complex of shrines is included in the travel itineraries of these foreign guests, promoted as an unusual Shinto site. Hokkaido Shrine is seeing many *ema* (votive tablets on which prayers are written and displayed on the grounds of a shrine) written in Thai, and amongst the boxes selling *omikuji* fortune-telling strips is one labeled "Taiwanese language." Pamphlets giving the history of the shrines and explanations of various amulets on sale are available in English, Mandarin, Hangul, and many other languages.

As you can see, modern-day visitors to Hokkaido Shrine have no connection to the defense of the Northern Territories or to the settling of Hokkaido. They are coming for reasons other than the stories and perspectives provided by the shrines themselves. Visitors come because they have read in magazines or seen on television that they can go to Hokkaido Shrine and receive "power." To get this energy, they walk around the shrines, and hug the gingko and cedar trees or hold out their hands to them. The qi or mysterious force they are seeking is from a brand-new concept linked to the world of Shinto.

From the perspective of the organization that governs a particular shrine, this type of activity can be surprising and worrisome. Modern visitors see and read random information about religion. They take the parts they like and assemble them, a trend that appears strange to traditional believers. Consciously or unconsciously, and influenced perhaps by the media, people in today's society are turning more and more to privatized

Boxes selling fortune-telling strips of paper at Hokkaido Shrine. The right box is labeled "Taiwanese language."

religion. In the past, tourism-oriented "pilgrims" were not taken seriously. They were, in fact, considered a kind of noise that had a detrimental effect on holy ground.

However, to consider modern pilgrims influenced by secularization and privatization, we need a perspective that includes them because these new visitors are changing sacred places. We can also see situations where traditional believers and new pilgrims are having an influence on each other. Pilgrimages to sacred places are taking place in a context of tension between traditional believers and individuals with privatized faith. These pilgrimages are also merged with tourism. To discuss the nuances of sacred-spot tourism when mentioning modern pilgrimages, I have combined the language of the religious side with that of the secular side to emphasize the overlapping. While many religious organizations and systems continue to protect traditional beliefs, individuals are no longer satisfied with convention, and they carry out religious practices based on their own preferences. As a result, religious pilgrimages come to be treated in the same way as regular tourism. Thus religion is being reborn in a new form.

Definitions of religion and tourism

Let's take a quick look at the definition of religion. Basically there are as many definitions as there are researchers. This means the definition depends on who is speaking, and participants in a discussion on this subject often seem out of sync with each other. Even so, definitions of religion can be divided into two large categories: substantive definition and functional definition.

Substantive definition is focused on concrete constructs. For example, French sociologist Yves Lambert gives three conditions for a religion: the first is a power and presence that exceed human comprehension; the second is a method of communicating with that presence; the third is a community that supports the other two conditions (Lambert 2004). In other words, this perspective says that a religion is a group of believers. This is perhaps the definition closest to generally held perceptions.

Substantive definitions of religion are easy to understand, but have some problems. They do not allow, for example, fortune telling and therapy to be considered religions. Neither necessarily involves a god or other deity, and they are not necessarily part of religious organizations. For the same reasons, visiting power spots would not be considered a religious activity. In an increasingly secular and privatized society, however, along with a growth in the type of spirituality mentioned earlier in this chapter, something akin to religion has been created at these power spots, despite a lack of organization. There may be no deity involved, but there are people who feel an amazing strength, energy, and power, and they are the ones making modern-day pilgrimages.

To understand this new sort of religious sensitivity and practice, a more flexible point of view is required. Let's examine a functional definition of religion. This definition says that a religion has a specific function, but it need not involve a church or organization. This perspective allows us to see aspects of religion in many different parts of society.

Different people find different functions for religion in their lives, but one of the most common is "finding meaning." J. Milton Yinger defines religion as a "system of beliefs and practices by means of which a group of people struggles with . . . the ultimate problems of human life" (Yinger 1970).

A person's interpretation of the world can change when a coincidence is given meaning and perceived as necessary. In other words, shifting the framework of our interpretation of the world is a function of religion. On the path of life, humans often incur unforeseeable unhappiness and misfortune. They may lose a loved one in an accident or become seriously ill themselves. Tragic events befall us in random ways. Science can explain the actual accident or disease, but it cannot explain the timing and why it happened to us. Sudden tragedy, however, can be endured if it is given meaning and becomes part of a story. Disease and loss can be viewed positively as opportunities from God to reassess life.

Religion, when defined as having the function of giving meaning to things, doesn't need an organization. Now we can see religious aspects in therapy and fortune telling, and anything else that promotes healing or puts energy back into a person's life, including a vacation to a sacred site.

In this book, we will use the word "religion" flexibly with both substantive and functional definitions. If we only think substantively, we will be limited to connecting sacred places to the stories told by organized religions. This will give holy places value only to passionate believers. If we think about functional aspects, on the other hand, we can discuss them as places with meaning even for nonbelievers. At all times, we must bear in mind that many different types of individuals use various methods to access religious things, and these are not limited to following the teachings of religious organizations.

Finally, in this introduction let us look at the definition of tourism, a key theme of this book. Its meaning can be as varied as that of religion. Hashimoto Kazuya, a prominent tourism anthropologist, defines tourism as "going to a strange land and conducting transactions for a tiny piece of something well known to temporarily enjoy." He offered the definition in an attempt to clarify an outline of tourism as a relatively new object of research. Hashimoto differentiates tourism from other phenomena in terms of temporality, entertainment, and monetary transactions. When distinguishing pilgrimages from tourism, he points out that even "imitations" are included in tourism. He ascertains that tourists will pay money to go to reconstructions and copies of things and derive enjoyment from them. Religious pilgrimages do not include such counterfeits, he claims (Hashimoto 1999). This makes Hashimoto appear critical of tourism, but his intention is to put the subject in as specific a position as possible.

The basic perspective of this book is as follows: due to secularization, religion is drawing further away from the forefront of society. Therefore this book will focus on both substantive and functional definitions of religion. I want to consider religion broadly enough to find it even in secular fields.

On the other hand, I am using as reference Hashimoto's narrow definition of tourism. In modern society, tourism, unlike organized religion, is increasing and becoming more widespread. As religion appears to be disappearing, tourism has become a more familiar presence. I'd like to begin with a definition as narrow as possible, using the concepts of temporality, leisure, and transactions.

The purpose of this book, however, is not to separate religion and tourism. It is to discuss the cultural changes taking place at the intersection of the two. When tourism works its way into religion or religion is brought into tourism, it becomes impossible to separate the two, and we end up with a sort of fusion that cannot be referred to as either one or the other.

Chapter outlines

In this book, we will be examining specific cases of the fusion of religious pilgrimages and tourism. Although the word *fusion* is used to describe them all, they are diverse in nature. For example, when religion is built into a tourist destination, the context can vary greatly depending on whether the destination is government managed (such as a World Heritage site, for example) or a privately promoted "power spot." It also depends on the doctrine of the particular religion being linked to that destination. We will look at examples of these different types of contexts by making our own pilgrimage to sacred places that combine religion and tourism and examining them from different vantage points.

In chapter 1, we will take a broad look at the characteristics of pilgrimages in a secular society using as clues the characteristics of sacred Catholic places involving relics and apparitions of the Virgin Mary. What do these clues tell us about the expectations of visitors to sacred places? We will also consider the importance of authenticity.

In chapter 2 we will look at pilgrimages to Santiago de Compostela in order to discuss the increase of "nonreligious pilgrims." The Camino de Santiago pilgrimage leads to the cathedral built in honor of Saint James. The well-known route has a history beginning in the Middle Ages. Each year, over a hundred thousand people make the trip on foot, but the numbers have been this high only since the beginning of the twenty-first century. The majority of pilgrims, who walk a distance of up to a thousand kilometers (about six hundred miles) to complete this task, almost never go to church. Why then, do they decide to do it? Talking to the pilgrims and observing their experiences, we can see that human interaction—not religion—is the sought-after element in this trek.

In chapter 3, we will look at nonreligious authorities and systems and consider their influence on traditional religious culture, with particular reference to the World Heritage system. Trade-offs are used to decide whether or not the World Heritage label can be granted, and if so, where it should be attached. World Heritage is a nonreligious authority, and its influence brings a new hierarchy into play that changes religious culture. I want to focus on the process of how holy sites and their images are "edited" as a result of trade-offs made by stakeholders, including local governments, local citizens, the media, and so on as they strive to gain World Heritage status.

The case study in chapter 4 is about the legend that Jesus Christ is buried in a tomb in Aomori Prefecture in northern Japan. We will look at the process of how a place with no historical or academic background becomes sacred. The story of the tomb of Christ was based on a mysterious legend that sprang up in the years leading to World War II. The tomb is considered a second-rate tourist attraction that appeals to those with an interest in the supernatural. The people living in the area don't consider the tomb authentic, and yet they have embraced it as part of their culture. The tomb of Christ, an admittedly radical case, will be analyzed in terms of community support for sacred spots. We will learn that for a sacred spot to continue to have importance, the subjective experiences and emotions of the people involved with it are as important as evaluation based on objective knowledge and values.

Holy places can also change due to word-of-mouth, media attention, and other secular forces. There are cases of sacred spots changing voluntarily to meet the demands of those who visit them. Chapter 5 will deal with examples of these, namely the power-spot boom in Japan that began in the first years of the twenty-first century. Behind this boom is the rise of a new religious sensitivity that emphasizes personal interests and preferences. In the privatized society, existing religions fail to satisfy people, who then create and act on their own style of beliefs. Power spots are a clear example of this.

When we look at the crossroads of religion and tourism in today's world, we can see that religion is taking on new forms and these new forms are penetrating many different aspects of society. In the final chapter of this book, I will present a theoretical framework for the consideration of modern-day holy places based on the discussion thus far. We will look at the example of Washinomiya Shrine, a forerunner for so-called anime sacred-spot pilgrimages, and consider the increase in event-type sacred spots in a secular society.

Pilgrimages are an opportunity to create community in a society in which personal interests and values have become extremely diversified. From sacred sites can grow a sense of identity and belonging for the people who live around and visit them. Using these examples, I want to give a glimpse of the ways in which the position of religion is changing in today's society.

Chapter 1

Looking for Holy Things: What Do Pilgrims See?

People travel to certain places because something draws them there. These places distinguish themselves with sights or experiences not on offer elsewhere. In this chapter, we will take a look at what can be called the "attractions" of sacred places. Attractions may come in the form of clothing or other items used by God or a saint or some other object that offers proof of a miracle. Believers head for holy sites so they can stand before these relics and pray. What do they mean, though, for people without faith? Taking it to an extreme, an object of worship for the faithful may be nothing but junk to someone who doesn't believe in the religion.

This is a logical conclusion, but the fact remains that people, religious or not, go to sacred places in droves. In this chapter, we will examine the attractions at sacred spots to figure out what makes a pilgrimage worthwhile to nonreligious pilgrims. I'd like to do this by introducing the concept of authenticity.

The world of holy relics

Attractions in holy places vary depending on the religion, the region, and the age. In fact, it is impossible to discuss them as a whole. Here, I'd like to look mainly at the attractions of holy places of the Roman Catholic Church in Western Europe, a region where social secularization and religious privatization are clearly in evidence.

To begin with, most sacred sites of the Roman Catholic Church have holy relics, often the remains or a few bones of saints or people mentioned in the Bible, or things believed to have been touched by these people. The most important holy relics have a direct connection to Jesus

Christ, such as bits of cloth from his clothing, the crown of thorns placed on his head, the nails hammered through his hands and feet on the cross, the lance of the Roman soldier that pierced him in the side (the Lance of Longinus), and burial shrouds used to wrap Jesus' body after his death, some of which have spots of his blood on them. There are also relics believed to be pieces of the cross on which Christ died.

Among the more unusual items is the sanctuary that holds the Scala Santa, or Holy Stairs, in Rome. It is said that the stairs were brought from the praetorium, or palace, of Pontius Pilate, the governor who sentenced Jesus to death. Legend has it that Jesus walked up and down the stairs before he was nailed to the cross. Today, pilgrims come to the Scala Santa and pray as they reverently climb the stairs on their knees.

Innumerable relics exist in churches all over the world, including the skull of Mary Magdalene, who watched Jesus die on the cross and was one of the first to discover the resurrected Christ; the chains that held Saint Peter, who was nailed to a cross upside down by Emperor Nero; and the remains of Saint James, one of the Twelve Apostles of Jesus, which were discovered at Santiago de Compostela in Spain, turning the location into a sacred place worthy of pilgrimage, and whose significance we will look at more closely in chapter 2. There are also relics that have

People praying on the Scala Santa in Rome.

no direct connection to Jesus, such as a clump of blood from Saint Janarius that supposedly turns into liquid on holy days and some of the hairs from the head and beard of Friar Maximilian Maria Kolbe (1894–1941), who volunteered to die in the place of another prisoner at the Auschwitz death camp during World War II. The sheer number and diversity of relics connected to Catholicism in countries throughout the world attest to the reach of this faith.

Beautiful containers, called reliquaries, are made to hold the precious relics. The relics themselves are not esthetically pleasing, so the reliquaries are adorned with gems and precious metals. In the Louvre in Paris, there is an entire exhibit devoted to these reliquaries. A bust of Francisco Xavier, the missionary who brought Christianity to Japan, is kept in St. Mary's Cathedral of Sekiguchi Catholic Church in Tokyo. The bust, a gift from Germany, was actually designed as a reliquary.

In the world of the Catholic religion, holy relics create a physical link between a place and the Supreme Being, and bestow sanctity on that place. According to Patrick J. Geary, the dead bodies and other relics of saints were at one time central to the religious world. Holy relics conferred status on both their towns and their owners. If a place had a relic, pilgrims would come from all over to see it. This allure endowed these bones and pieces of cloth and wood with political and economic power (Geary 1994).

During the Middle Ages, rich and powerful people, such as the French royal family and the Medicis, spent fortunes on acquiring relics. They then built churches and cathedrals to house them. Sainte-Chapelle in Paris, a Gothic-style royal chapel considered one of the most beautiful of its kind, was built by Louis IX to house Jesus' crown of thorns and the cross he was crucified on. Note that much more was spent to buy the relics than to build the cathedral. The Basilica of the Holy Blood in Bruges, Belgium, has a cloth soaked in what is claimed to be—as the name implies—the blood of Christ. Even today, the cloth is brought out several times a day to be viewed by tourists and other visitors.

Back in the Middle Ages there were merchants who specialized in relics. As you can imagine, and judging from the sheer numbers still in existence today, many of the so-called holy items have turned out to be fakes.

There are still in existence several lances that supposedly pierced the side of Christ as he hung on the cross, and, in France alone, multiple skulls of Mary Magdalene. It has been said, only half jokingly, that if all the pieces claimed to be from the cross of Christ were assembled in one place, there would be enough material to build a skyscraper.

Holy relics are considered to fall into three classes. The first class is for objects associated with the Passion (i.e., the suffering and death) of Christ, and also for a part of the body of a saint. Second-class relics are items used by saints or that they came into contact with. The third class is anything, such as a piece of cloth or a medal that has come into direct contact with a first- or second-class relic. Third-class relics can often be obtained over the Internet.

According to Catholic doctrine, relics do not have supernatural powers. They are merely a way to draw people closer to the church. Being able to look at physical reminders of holy figures adds depth to faith. For many believers saying prayers before holy objects offers an experience much deeper than normal supplications, one they consider a short cut to miracles and redemption. Relics, therefore, are the attractions behind pilgrimages to places sacred to the Catholic Church.

Padre Pio and the Shroud of Turin

Let us look at two examples of holy relics that are popular attractions even today. The first is the remains of the Italian priest Padre Pio (1887–1968), a rare twentieth century example of someone who performed many miracles in his life. He is said to have healed the sick and was witnessed in multiple places at the exact same time. When Pope John Paul II (1920–2005) was still a seminary student, he met Padre Pio, who told the novice that he would some day become Pope.

During World War II, Padre Pio purportedly appeared in the skies before fighter planes headed on a bombing raid. Surprised pilots turned back without releasing their bombs. Padre Pio is also well known for exhibiting stigmata, a phenomenon in which a person's hands and feet develop wounds, which sometimes bleed, in the same places where Jesus was nailed to the cross. Padre Pio's palms were reported to have bled continuously for fifty years, beginning in his late twenties. The wounds were

Padre Pio.

apparently quite painful, but the scent of his blood was said to be as fragrant as perfume.

Canonization in the Catholic Church is not a simple process. With the exception of martyrs, proof of scientifically inexplicable miracles is required, and investigation of reported miracles is thorough. Many saints don't attain holy status until several hundred years after their death. Padre Pio was canonized with record speed. Pope John Paul II proclaimed him a saint in 2002. In 2008 his body was exhumed and shown to the public. Several hundred thousand pilgrims came to see it. The remains of Padre Pio are now at rest in southern Italy at the Sanctuary of Saint Pio of Pietrelcina, also known as Padre Pio Pilgrimage Church, making it one of the main pilgrimage sites in the region.

The second example of a relic that has drawn a great deal of attention in modern times is the Shroud of Turin. Legend has it that the body of the crucified Christ was wrapped in it. Like other holy relics, a number of these cloths are in existence, but the Shroud of Turin kept in the Cathedral of Saint John the Baptist in Turin, Italy, is the best known because it bears the negative image of a man's entire body.

During the twentieth century, a number of scientific tests were conducted on the shroud. The results varied, but all pointed to the cloth being made long after the age of Christ. But even if only dating back to the

The Shroud of Turin.

Middle Ages, the question remains: how did anyone manage to create the negative effect centuries before the invention of the camera? Some advocates say it was made by Leonardo da Vinci (Picknett and Prince 1995).

The debate over the shroud continues today. The Catholic Church has not commented on its authenticity, maintaining the stance that holy relics are a valid way to lead people to faith. In 2010, the Shroud of Turin was shown for the first time in a decade. Close to two million pilgrims came to see it over the course of several weeks, Pope Benedict XVI among them. In 2013, the shroud was shown on Italian television and an app entitled Shroud 2.0 was released to coincide with it. The app, which has proved to be quite popular, has high-definition photographs allowing the viewer a close-up examination of the holy cloth. This is one example of the value of relics: they are physical objects that satisfy our need to come closer to people in the Bible and the saints who followed them.

Apparitions of the Virgin Mary

For centuries, holy relics were at the center of Catholic holy places, and virtually all pilgrimages meant traveling to see them. This situation was altered in the late nineteenth century with a series of miraculous apparitions of the Virgin Mary.

The woman referred to as the Virgin Mary is, of course, Jesus' mother,

Mary. Catholics have long debated her position in the religion, but she is still venerated today as a kind of goddess. In many churches in France, statues of Mary are much larger than those of Jesus. In Italy, there was once a vote to determine the most popular holy person, and Mary came out ahead of her son.

Since the Middle Ages, there have been records of the appearance of this special favorite of the people in many different places. Mary has appeared in churches, monasteries, private homes, dreams, on the top of mountains, and in town centers—almost anywhere you could think of. When she comes, she is said to bring healing and messages. In the West, these apparitions started to become more frequent from the late nineteenth century onwards, during the dawn of modern society. They often took place in France.

One of the first of a series of apparitions during the modern age was at the Chapel of Our Lady of the Miraculous Medal (hereafter Chapel of the Medal) in Paris, France. The chapel is located in the seventh arrondissement of Paris, on Rue du Bac along the left bank of the River Seine. The building is called a church, but it is actually the chapel of a convent. Right next to the church is Bon Marché, said to be the world's first department store. In short, the first apparition of the Virgin Mary in the modern age was in a major Paris shopping area—not the locale for a holy site most of us would imagine. The apparition of Mary came to Catherine Labouré (1806–1876), a novice nun, who had already had several visions since joining the order of the Daughters of Charity. These included the heart of St. Vincent de Paul, founder of her order, and the figure of Christ the King.

The Virgin Mary first appeared to Labouré on the evening of November 27, 1830. As she prayed in the chapel, she saw Mary on top of a globe, with one foot on a snake and rays of light coming out of both of her hands. Labouré heard a voice saying, "These rays symbolize the graces I shed upon those who ask for them." Then she saw the following words in gold, surrounding the Virgin Mary: "O Mary, conceived without sin, pray for us who have recourse to thee." The vision seemed to rotate, and Labouré saw a circle of twelve stars, and a cross combined with the letter "M." Underneath were two hearts. Once again she heard words: "Have a

The Chapel of the Medal in Paris, France.

medal struck upon this model. All those who wear it, when it is blessed, will receive great graces."

In 1832, two thousand medals (named Miraculous Medals) were made depicting the image in Labouré's vision. There were reports that those who wore the medals were protected from accidents and disaster, cures began to abound for a cholera outbreak in Paris at the time, and nonbelievers had dramatic changes of heart. Pope Gregory XVI also received one of the medals. By 1839, more than ten million medals had been distributed. By 1876, when Labouré died, there were over one billion of them around the world. Friar Maximilian Maria Kolbe, canonized after his death at Auschwitz, actively promoted veneration of the Virgin Mary using the medals. In 1917, Kolbe vowed that he would devote his life to the Virgin Mary's work, and founded the evangelization movement the Knights of the Immaculata. Members of this group call the Miraculous Medals "missionary bullets," and all of them wear one even today.

Thus the world learned of a holy apparition in the backstreets of Paris through the medium of these medals. The result was that a chapel in a convent, usually a secluded place closed off to the world, was opened to the general public and is still open to this day. According to statistics this author received from the Chapel of the Medal, it receives more than two hundred thousand pilgrims a month, or an estimated 2.5 to 3 million per year.

Since Catherine Labouré's vision at the Chapel of the Medal, there have been many sightings of the Virgin Mary, mainly in Europe but also in other countries throughout the world, and most of them have become pilgrimage sites. Other major apparitions are described here.

Our Lady of La Salette (France, 1846)
On a mountain 1,800 meters (approximately 6,000 feet) high, a boy aged eleven and a girl of fifteen were minding cows when they saw the Virgin Mary sitting on a rock, crying. Mary called the children to her and gave them a warning about famine and war.

Our Lady of Lourdes (France, 1858)
Young Bernadette Soubirous was gathering firewood when she met the Virgin Mary in a cave. Mary told the girl about an underground spring beneath the cave. The spring was discovered and the water from it was said to have miraculous curative powers. Even today, many pilgrims with injuries or disease make their way to Lourdes to visit the spring. It is one of the best known of the Roman Catholic holy sites.

Our Lady of Pontmain (France, 1871)
During the Franco-Prussian War, several children were working in a barn when they saw the Virgin Mary in the sky over one of the houses in their village. The adults who heard the children shouting and came out to see what was happening were unable to see the apparition. Words appeared in the sky, a message from Mary that the war would soon be over and the young people from the village who had been drafted into the army would be returning.

Apparition in Knock (Ireland, 1879)
The Virgin Mary, flanked by Saint Joseph and Saint John, appeared at the local church in the village of Knock. They were seen by fifteen people, aged five to over seventy. This apparition was unusual in that there was such a wide range of witnesses. Knock is one of the most important holy spots in Ireland, and has been visited by both Pope John Paul II and Mother Theresa.

Our Lady of Fátima (Portugal, 1917)

Three children near the town of Fátima saw the Virgin Mary multiple times, and she entrusted them with three messages, the last of which, known as The Third Prophecy of Fátima, was not to be opened until 1960. The messages have been interpreted as referring to the ending of World War I and also to the end of the world.

In addition to the examples listed above there are innumerable other reports of apparitions. At the end of the 1960s the Virgin Mary is said to have made several appearances over a church in Cairo, Egypt, surrounded by shining light. Photographs and videos of the apparition can be seen on the Internet. In Medjugorje, a town in Bosnia and Herzegovina, she appeared to a group of children in 1981 and has reportedly been seen there on other occasions since. The children who originally saw the vision are now adults, but claim to still receive messages from Mary, all of which are reported monthly on their website.

While it may be slightly different from an apparition, in 1973 a wooden image of the Virgin Mary in a convent in the city of Akita in Japan was seen shedding tears. The nun who saw it received a message from Mary and developed stigmata on her hands.

The two sides of the apparitions of the Virgin Mary

A display of relics, along with a history of appearances made by the Virgin Mary are both attractions of holy sites, but they are very different. Relics have material substance, while apparitions are nonmaterial phenomena. Apparitions do not require anything concrete to be passed down through generations. Not only that, but they can occur anywhere, often on the say-so of children, and only require a broad social acceptance to establish themselves (Seki 1993). Compared with holy relics, which are static and concrete, apparitions are dynamic pilgrimage attractions. For the church, though, they are a double-edged sword.

On the one hand, the impact of dynamic miracles like holy apparitions brings many pilgrims from secular society. This is a good thing for the church. Over five million pilgrims a year make their way to Lourdes. Since the spring water in Lourdes is said to have the power to cure, many

People at Lourdes.

of the pilgrims are injured or sick. At the site are volunteers to assist these visitors (Terado 2006).

Many of the Lourdes volunteers are not Christian believers, but by helping the injured and sick, they have an opportunity to consider their own lives and many learn to look at things in a new way. France is very strict about separating church and state, but there are many schools that send their students to Lourdes to help out as a part of school trips. From this we can see that because of Lourdes, a holy place, the Catholic Church is finding a new place for itself in a secular society.

On the other hand, the fact that the Virgin Mary could appear anywhere means that holy places can also pop up anywhere, and this has potential danger for the church. The Roman Catholic Church has over one billion members throughout the world, and the center of the Catholic world is the Pope in the Vatican. Serving as an agent of God, the Pope is at the top of the organization that unifies the world's Catholics.

The Virgin Mary, with her ability to appear anywhere, could become a threat to conventional Catholic authority. For example, during apparitions, Mary often criticizes the way the Catholic Church is run and sends messages that involve conflicts and politics, which could be a risk to the church. It is no surprise, therefore, that very few of the appearances made by the Virgin Mary are officially recognized.

The authenticity of holy things

So far we have looked at two types of holy-site attractions: relics, and apparitions of the Virgin Mary. They do not represent all possible attractions, but they serve as guidelines to thinking about attractions in general.

There are Buddhist attractions that correspond almost exactly to Catholic relics. *Busshari*, for example, are said to be ashes, bones, and even hair from the body of the Buddha. They are preserved in Buddhist temples all over Japan and are considered objects of worship. In the introduction to this book, we read about the daily food offerings made to Kukai at Mount Koya. These offerings are not in themselves sacred; rather it is Kukai, as the real presence of a supreme being, who supports the sacrality of the place. This could be said to correspond to visions of the Virgin Mary.

Let's go back to the main point of this chapter: how the attractions—relics and visions—of pilgrimages are accepted in secular society. What do they mean to nonbelievers who visit holy places?

People head for holy sites to see something special. They wouldn't go if the attractions were available elsewhere. For people who believe in miracles, however, the existence of multiple crowns of thorns and lances of Longinus are proof that all but one of each item (if not all) are counterfeits. The same is true for apparitions of the Virgin Mary; they can be accepted only by those who believe in them.

To nonbelievers, relics and apparitions are no more than fiction created by religion. Yet, people without faith make visits to holy sites. Have they made peace with the fact that what they've come to see is a hoax? There has got to be more to it than that. These "pilgrims" must get value from the experience that is separate from religion.

As we consider this issue, I want to further discuss the concept of authenticity to help us gain insights into the experiences of nonbelievers visiting holy sites.

The authenticity of Shurijo Castle

Let's explore the concept of authenticity by looking at some tourist attractions that are not places of religious pilgrimage, such as Shurijo Castle in Okinawa, Japan (Plate 10). This castle was the home of the rulers of the Ryukyu Kingdom (the ancient name for Okinawa before it became part of Japan), and was the control center for the kingdom's government and military. It also functioned as a religious center, with an important holy site (*utaki*), in its grounds. The castle building was extensively damaged twice, and no longer has the same structure as when the rulers of the kingdom lived there.

The castle was first damaged in 1879 during a period of conflict known as the Ryuku Disposition, when the new Japanese government that came to power as a result of the Meiji Revolution in 1868 decided to annex the Ryukyu Islands, giving them the name Okinawa Prefecture. Soldiers sent there by the Meiji government surrounded the castle, deposed the king, and took up residence. During this occupation and the castle's subsequent use as a school, much remodeling took place, such as the addition of windows and the knocking down of walls. This meant that most of the castle's original structure was destroyed.

At the beginning of the twentieth century, the architect Ito Chuta (1867–1954) carried out repairs to Shurijo, after which its State Chamber was designated a Japanese national treasure. In other words, its value as a cultural property was confirmed. During the Pacific War (1941–1945), however, the castle was once again destroyed. The Japanese Thirty-second Army had been assigned to Okinawa in the closing days of the war to prepare for the landing of the American army. The Japanese command center occupied an underground bunker dug below Shurijo Castle. American attacks on the center completely demolished the castle.

After the war, the site of the castle became the Ryukyu University campus. In the 1980s the university completed its move to a new site and the Shurijo Castle Restoration Project, whose aim was to restore the castle to its pre–Meiji Revolution state, went into full swing. By that time, almost all of the records of how the castle looked as well as the techniques used to decorate it had been lost. The rebuilding of the castle we see today was possible thanks to the meticulous investigations of many historians and artisans.

In other words, the present-day Shurijo is not the original castle. In 2000, when the Gusuku Sites and Related Properties of the Kingdom of Ryukyu were added to the UNESCO World Cultural Heritage List, the site of the original castle was included, but not the building itself, because it was a restoration.

When considering the history of Shurijo Castle, however, it feels wrong to label the attraction as a counterfeit. Despite the fact that almost everything was destroyed during World War II, the reconstruction project managed to verify details about roof tiles and other materials used to construct the original castle. The characteristic red color was not visible in black and white photos, but thorough investigations were made to ensure authenticity. In other words, the present-day Shurijo Castle is an almost perfect reproduction of the one built during the Ryukyu Kingdom period.

By restoring Shurijo Castle to look as it did when it was the center of politics, religion and the military, it became a symbol of Okinawa. This was the intent of the restoration project. This is also what has made it an attraction people from other parts of the country want to visit.

The authenticity of restored castle towers

Let's look at another example. Many Japanese enjoy visiting castles, a pastime referred to as "history sightseeing." Castles with beautiful towers are considered symbols of Japanese culture and are top tourist attractions, not just for Japanese but for foreign visitors too.

Very few castle towers, however, are preserved in their original state. Twelve castles in Japan, including Himeji and Hikone, have towers said to be original, but most others have been repaired and rebuilt, and are referred to as "restored" or "reconstructed." Some are fortified with concrete; other restorations are more like educated guesses because there are few historical documents to work from. Kumamoto Castle, with its distinctive black castle walls, has very little about it that can be called original—including its towers and its great hall—due to damage sustained during the Satsuma Rebellion in 1877 and an earthquake in 1889. The castle was restored after these incidents but was once again greatly damaged in an earthquake in 2016, and it is estimated that repairs will take twenty years. No one, though, would consider this work as the construction of a counterfeit. Moreover, the newly restored castle is bound to be a stronger symbol of the area than before.

So, a visit to a castle often means visiting a *reproduction* of a castle. If we assume visitors fail to get an authentic experience, however, we would be mistaken. Even if buildings are reconstructions, they still offer contact with Japanese culture. People living close to castle towers that have been beautifully reconstructed must be proud to claim them as a local symbol.

For a case somewhat different from Shurijo, let's look at the reconstruction of Nagoya Castle. This fortress played a key role at important junctures in Japanese history, especially during the Warring States period (1467–1568). Almost all of the original structure, though, was burned to the ground in US air raids during World War II. The castle on view today was built of fortified concrete on a steel frame in 1959.

In 2009, when seismic reinforcement was planned, the mayor began a movement to completely rebuild the castle in wood to restore it to a condition closer to its original state in order to better promote tourism. One interesting aspect of the process was the questionnaire sent out to the citizens of Nagoya. They were asked whether the concrete castle towers should be reinforced as they were, or torn down and rebuilt in wood, restoring them to their original state. More than 70 percent responded in favor of reinforcing the existing concrete towers.

These results can be interpreted in the light of a number of issues, including the cost of complete restoration. What we can say for certain, however, is that restoring something to its original state is not always the most popular move, even for a castle that represents a whole city. In Nagoya, it is the concrete reproduction castle, built after the war, that people want to preserve.

Creating holy sites: a diversity of authenticity

After examining the stories of Shurijo Castle and of reproduction castle towers in Japan, it is clear that there is a very fuzzy line between the authentic and the counterfeit. From academic and historical viewpoints, it is easy to judge an attraction as either one or the other. When an attraction is fabricated, however, the provider and the visitor do not regard it as a fake attraction.

As restoration of Shurijo Castle shows, the intention of the attraction's provider—that the castle should be a symbol of modern-day Okinawa—is important. In addition, however, we must consider the experience of visitors and the value they give to the attraction. We can say, therefore, that we must carefully analyze not just how an attraction is "edited" and reconstructed by the provider, but also how it is accepted by the visitor.

In this analysis we started by looking at the characteristics of authenticity as related to religious pilgrimages to holy sites of the Roman Catholic Church. For believers, there is nothing fictional about these holy relics or apparitions. They are all authentic objects and events recognized by the church, whose authority they trust. For members of the faith, relics stored in sacred places have neither archeological nor historical significance. They are authentic according to the institution of the church.

Yet the authenticity of some relics and apparitions is difficult to verify. From a scientific viewpoint, most of them could be written off as fakes. So why then do these attractions draw visitors who are not believers? These tourists do not accept holy relics as holy. Nor do they think of visions of the Mother Mary as miracles. Yet still they come.

Let's listen to what Yamanaka Hiroshi, a leading authority on religion and tourism, has to say: "Tourism is a form of consumption behavior in which an area or various different things in the area are presented as worth visiting, and based on this presentation, people from outside of the area travel there to fulfill their own diversified demands. This has a great deal to do with uniqueness and unusualness" (Yamanaka 2009).

Yamanaka draws our attention to the fact that some attractions are created for the sake of visitors. The reason why people go to these sacred places or tourist spots is merely because there is something to see there that is not available elsewhere. This "uniqueness" or "unusualness" as described by Yamanaka varies from place to place. Certain tourist sites have been produced and modified for effect. In other words, the attractions have been edited to stimulate the desire of visitors to see it. Sacred sites and attractions that have been certified as authentic by religious authorities are being recreated due to the increase in nonreligious visitors in a secularized society.

Earlier in this chapter, I introduced the theory of how in recent years the Shroud of Turin has been suspected of being the work of Leonardo da Vinci. This is one example of how a piece of cloth considered to be holy has been "re-produced" as the work of a historically prominent artist, giving it new value that has made it interesting to a secularized society.

In the next chapters, we will look more closely at examples of how nonreligious visitors get meaning out of sacred sites and achieve authentic experiences. Even if a person does not believe in the conventional religious meaning of a place, they can read their own story into it. This sort of "privatization" of religion is making great changes to sacred spots.

In a secular society, it is simplistic to suggest that an attraction in a holy place must be either fake or authentic based on history and scholarship. Attractions are modified and recreated to make them worth seeing, and in these intentionally produced attractions, visitors are able to find meaning and have valuable experiences.

From the Goal to the Process: Non-believer Pilgrims Keep on Walking

Pilgrimages to the Cathedral of Santiago de Compostela in Spain (Plate 4) began in the Middle Ages. Since the beginning of the twenty-first century the Camino de Santiago pilgrimage has increased dramatically in popularity to become one of the busiest pilgrimage routes in the world.

Interestingly, most of the pilgrims are not regular churchgoers. Many of them come from parts of the world where Christianity is not the dominant religion. They are people who do not have the faith of Saint James, a disciple of Christ, to whom the Santiago cathedral is dedicated. Why, then, do these people walk the pilgrimage route? What meaning or authentic experience do they get from their journey? Today's Camino de Santiago pilgrimage is a perfect example for the consideration of religious pilgrimages in a secular society.

The history of the Camino de Santiago pilgrimage
Saint James, one of the twelve disciples of Christ, is said to have been martyred in about 44 AD. Legend has it that two fellow disciples spirited his body away from Jerusalem in a stone boat, looking for somewhere to give him a decent burial. They landed in Spain and buried Saint James there.

In the ninth century, bones believed to be those of Saint James were discovered on the Iberian Peninsula. In 813, a hermit called Pelagius saw a mysterious light that led him to the tomb. Pelagius notified a bishop, Teodomiro, that he had discovered a holy place. At first a small church was built to commemorate the spot, and the first recorded pilgrimage to it was in 950 by the French priest Godescalc of Le Puy-en-Velay (whose cathedral has been a UNESCO World Heritage site since 1998, as part of the "Routes of Santiago de Compostela in France").

Later in the ninth century, when Christians were battling to take back the Iberian Peninsula from the Moors, a legend spread that Saint James, dressed as a knight and riding on a white horse, came to the aid of the Christians, who were losing to the Moors, and led them to victory. The legend of Saint James Matamoros, or Saint James the Moor-slayer, made the disciple extremely popular. Paintings and sculptures of him are different from those of other saints in that he often carries a sword and is pictured in battle.

In the eleventh and twelfth centuries, pilgrimages to Rome and Jerusalem became dangerous due to the Byzantine–Seljuq wars, a series of conflicts between the European Byzantine Empire and the Turkish Seljuq dynasty. In their place, pilgrimages to Santiago became popular. In the thirteenth and fourteenth centuries, monastic orders such as the Order of Saint Benedict and the Congregation of Cluny, as well as various chivalric orders maintained the pilgrimage route and built facilities along the way for pilgrims. At its peak, five hundred thousand pilgrims a year made the trek (Seki 2006).

With a history going back to the Middle Ages, the Santiago pilgrimage is frequently referred to as a traditional one. The facts, however, show that the number of people who made the journey declined precipitously during the years of the Black Death plague in the fourteenth century as well as during the Hundred Years' War of the fourteenth and fifteenth centuries. The sixteenth century brought the Anglo–Spanish War. When the English attacked the Galician coast, where Santiago is located, the remains of Saint James were hidden to protect them, but were lost in the process.

July 25 was proclaimed Saint James Day by Pope Callixtus II in 1122. Over the centuries, however, fewer and fewer pilgrims made the trip. As recently as the middle of the nineteenth century only a few dozen bothered to go to Santiago even on July 25.

The remains of Saint James were missing until 1879. A search project conducted in Santiago under the auspices of the Archbishop of Santiago finally found them on the site of the church that had been built in honor of the missing saint. In 1884, Pope Leo XIII recognized these remains as those of Saint James, but even this failed to make the Santiago church popular as a pilgrimage destination. In the saint's Jubilee year (a year when his holy day falls on a Sunday) of 1982, Pope John Paul II made a pilgrimage to Santiago, but in the years that followed few believers made the trip. The total for 1986 was said to be less than two thousand five hundred.

The number of pilgrims to Santiago began to grow during the mid-1990s after Brazilian novelist Paulo Coelho wrote the book *The Pilgrimage* drawing on his own experiences. When Coelho's later novels became bestsellers, *The Pilgrimage* was translated into many different languages and read throughout the world. In 2000, American actress Shirley MacLaine wrote *The Camino: A Journey of the Spirit*, the story of her own pilgrimage to Santiago.

What should be stressed here is that neither Coelho nor MacLaine wrote their stories from the viewpoint of a devout Catholic. The main character of Coelho's book belongs to a secret organization and fails a

Pilgrims praying before the remains of Saint James.

test for promotion. To make up for this, he is sent on the Camino de Santiago pilgrimage to look for a symbolic sword. Along the route, the character is required to undergo training in various places, to learn what he needs to know.

MacLaine is well-known for her participation in the New Age movement and has declared herself a devotee of the Eastern belief of transmigration of the soul. As might be expected, MacLaine's pilgrimage to Santiago, as described in *The Camino*, describes one mystical experience after another, including encounters with her previous incarnations and her guardian spirit.

There are also a number of well-known films about the Camino de Santiago pilgrimage, including *Saint-Jacques . . . la Mecque* (Saint James . . . Mecca; France, 2005) and *The Way* (US–Spain, 2010). The former is about three non-Catholic siblings who make the pilgrimage together. The elder brother runs a company and thinks about nothing but his job, the sister teaches French and hates religion, and the younger brother is an unemployed alcoholic. Their mother has stipulated in her will that they must make the pilgrimage in order to inherit her estate. The three make the journey, meeting up along the way with a group of teenagers who are not even aware that the hiking tour they are on is a pilgrimage route. The film touches on religious issues facing France while questioning whether there is a place or even a need for religion in French society, where the Catholic Church has lost its influence.

The Way stars Martin Sheen as an older man making the pilgrimage. In this film, too, the main character is not making the trip because he wants to. His son has dropped out of graduate school to rebel against his father and sets out along the Camino de Santiago to find himself. Soon after the son begins the trip, however, he has an accident and dies in the Pyrenees. The character played by Sheen decides to make the trip himself, scattering his son's ashes along the way. By the end of the film, the father has learned to empathize with his son's bohemian values, and sets out on another trip, this time around the world. Once again, this movie has a perspective far removed from that of the Catholic faith.

These books and films are frequently mentioned by pilgrims as their introduction to the Camino de Santiago pilgrimage as well as the motivation for embarking on it. The works by Coelho and MacLaine especially, are regarded as modern-day Santiago bibles and are widely considered to have contributed to the sudden increase in pilgrims at the end of the twentieth century. Both books describe how the main characters underwent spiritual and moral changes, but neither of them is written from a traditional Catholic viewpoint.

We must also bear in mind that this pilgrimage route was registered as a UNESCO Cultural World Heritage site in 1993. This increased awareness of the Camino de Santiago has put it on the tourism map as a place of Christian historical interest. In 1993, a Jubilee year for Saint James, close to one hundred thousand pilgrims made the trek.

The graph below shows the number of pilgrims who received certificates stating that they had met the church's criteria for successfully completing the pilgrimage (as explained on pp. 65–66). The graph shows a steady increase in recent years, with numbers spiking during Jubilee years. In 2001, the annual number of pilgrims exceeded 50,000. Since 2006, it has been over 100,000. Each Jubilee year, a new record is set: 180,000 in 2004, followed by over 270,000 in 2010. The number of pilgrims receiving certificates in 2017 exceeded 300,000, more than one hundred times the figure for 1987 (2,905), even though 2017 was not a Jubilee year.

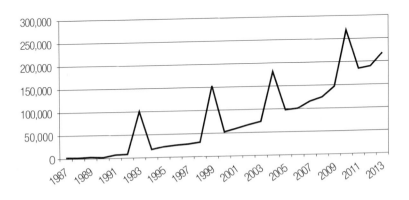

Figure 1:
Annual number of pilgrims to Santiago (1987-2013). Compiled by the author based on statistics from the Pilgrim's Reception Office.

Thus we can see how the Camino de Santiago pilgrimage began to flourish at the end of the twentieth century, thanks to secular books and films and the acknowledgement of UNESCO, a secular organization.

Camino de Santiago pilgrimages today

Let's take a look at how modern-day pilgrims travel the Camino de Santiago. As you can see from the map below, some well-known routes begin in France, such as those from Tours, Limoges, Le Puy, and Toulouse. To walk these routes means a total trip of two to three months. A shorter and much more popular route is the Camino Francés (the French Way), which begins in Saint Jean Pied de Port (hereafter Saint Jean) near the Spanish border, giving pilgrims the chance to climb the Pyrenees, and then passes through Pamplona, Burgos, León, and Astorga. About 70 percent of all pilgrims take this route.

In Europe there are many cases of people making the journey from home on foot. Among the people this author met was a Swiss woman who left her home in Geneva and headed first in the opposite direction of Santiago, all the way to the eastern tip of Switzerland, from where she began her walk west. Then there was a Swedish couple in their sixties, traveling from Stockholm. The husband ran, and the wife accompanied him on a bicycle.

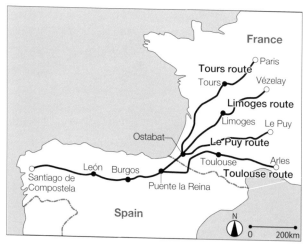

Figure 2:
Pilgrimage routes to Santiago.

There are three main categories of pilgrims. The largest category is walkers who carry a load usually no heavier than ten kilograms and cover fifteen to twenty kilometers (ten to twelve miles) a day, enjoying the nature and the Romanesque churches along the way (Plate 5). At night, these pilgrims can stay at bed-and-breakfasts in small villages. This category comes closest to popularly held perceptions of traditional pilgrimages. A trek starting at Saint Jean usually takes about forty days.

The next largest group is pilgrims traveling by bicycle. Much of the road is paved, so cyclists can travel over a hundred kilometers (about sixty miles) a day. They can make it to Santiago from Saint Jean in as little as ten days. When bicycles break down, riders have to fix it themselves, so this group consists mainly of bicycle hobbyists who are in it for the exercise. The third group is made up of a minority who make the pilgrimage on horse, donkey, with a guide dog, or in a wheelchair.

Looking at the statistics for 2017 from the Pilgrim's Reception Office (Oficina de Acogida al Peregrino) in Santiago, over half the pilgrims were under thirty. Those aged thirty to sixty made up 28 percent of pilgrims, while 7 percent were over sixty. The ratio of men to women was 51:49. About half of the pilgrims were from a country other than Spain (with more than 120 countries represented). The largest numbers of pilgrims from other countries were Germans (7.7 percent), Italians (7.6 percent), Portuguese (4.1 percent), French (4.1 percent), and Americans (3.5 percent), in that order.

According to the Catholic Bishops' Conference of Japan, as of 2017 there are approximately 440,000 Catholics in Japan. Not all of these are churchgoers, but nevertheless, the number of Japanese pilgrims to Santiago was 1,479 in 2017, which accounted for 0.4 percent of all pilgrims to Santiago that year. Considering the distance between Spain and Japan, and also the small number of Catholics in Japan, this is a remarkably large figure which indicates that many Japanese must make the pilgrimage with motivations other than religious faith.

Pilgrims who cover at least a hundred kilometers on foot or horseback to arrive in Santiago and bicyclists who travel two hundred kilometers or more receive the Compostela, the official document to certify that a pilgrimage has been made. When applying for this at the end of a journey, pilgrims are asked to choose one of three motivations: religious and others, religious, or nonreligious. The total for the first two is generally almost 90 percent, but cannot be taken at face value. Those who admit to making a nonreligious pilgrimage receive a "certificate of welcome" rather than a Compostela. This certificate is of simple design and can be obtained by anyone visiting Santiago—regardless of how they got there. Pilgrims will tell you they have made the journey for self-actualization, or to find themselves, or for leisure or sport, but so that they can receive the Compostela, most will say they had religious motivation.

The above statistics cover only pilgrims who have applied for the Compostela. Total visitors to Santiago are estimated at about 2.6 million in 2017. Some pilgrims are unable to make the entire journey in one go, and break it up into sections that are walked over a longer period of time. Others are backpacking or motorcycling around Europe and add part of the pilgrimage route to their itinerary. None of these categories are included in the Compostela statistics.

Pilgrims carry with them a credential, or "passport," in which they collect stamps from the places they visit along the way as proof of their journey. Churches, hostels, cafes, and restaurants on the route have stamps for pilgrims to put in their passports. When a journey is complet-

A pilgrim making the journey on a donkey.

ed, the passport and its stamps serve as proof that the distance has been properly covered.

Passports can be issued at some hostels and churches along the route, but many people get them through the branch pilgrim offices that exist in the United States, United Kingdom, Netherlands, France, Brazil, Japan, and other countries. These offices provide information about the pilgrimage as well as issuing passports. Some of the offices help maintain the route and run hostels for pilgrims.

Almost all pilgrims spend their nights at an *albergue* hostel exclusively for their use. Albergues are similar to youth hostels in that the basic facilities are bunk beds and showers, pilgrims have to check in during the afternoon and early evening, and lights have to be out by ten or eleven at night. Some albergues are run by government or religious organizations and some are private; the latter are more expensive. Priority for beds is given in this order: first walkers, then horse riders and finally bicyclists, and everyone must be out by seven or eight the next morning. The rule is one night only at any accommodation, unless a pilgrim is ill or injured. None of the albergues take reservations, so during the busy season, many pilgrims arrive in a village exhausted from their day's journey, but have nowhere to sleep and are obliged to travel several more kilometers to the next lodging.

More facilities for walking pilgrims are available each year as new cafes, restaurants, and albergues are built. There are even pilgrimage taxis to take your luggage ahead to the next planned stop. Travel agencies provide guided tours for walkers who cannot speak Spanish.

It is interesting how determined modern pilgrims are to make the journey on foot. These days there are flights to Santiago, as well as trains and highways. Why do people choose to go on foot, especially when they do not have religious faith? Why make such a simple trip so difficult?

As mentioned in chapter 1, the important thing about making a pilgrimage to a holy relic is being able to pray in front of it. Nonbelievers, one would assume, have little interest in prayer, so why go to the trouble of making the trip by the most inconvenient of all methods? The answer is that they have replaced the importance of the relic with the importance of the journey. In other words, these pilgrims have moved away from the goal of praying before the relic and have revived the once-abandoned process of getting there.

We see that the length of time required to make a pilgrimage has been intentionally extended. What sort of experience awaits the pilgrims on their lengthy journey? Interviews and innumerable written accounts of pilgrimages make it clear that a great deal of emphasis is placed on interpersonal exchange, in other words, meeting with and parting from people during the pilgrimage. When it comes to the Camino de Santiago pilgrimage, this aspect is illustrated by the role of the *hospitalero*, a short-term volunteer who helps run the albergue guesthouse and take care of pilgrims. These volunteers prepare meals, act as receptionists, do the cleaning and any other necessary work. Many hospitaleros have completed the pilgrimage multiple times and can give advice to pilgrims based on their own experiences.

When hospitaleros are assigned to an albergue, usually for a period of two weeks to a month, many of them use the opportunity to begin yet another pilgrimage, making sure to arrive at their guesthouse by the day they start work. When their stints end, they set off for Santiago, completing the journey. There are some foreign pilgrims who, after earning a number of Compostela certificates, move to Spain to become albergue operators.

Why are veteran pilgrims eager to become hospitaleros? Many of those that this author interviewed said that they wanted to go deeper into the world of pilgrimage and savor it. When asked why they thought they could achieve this by serving as a hospitalero, the answer was that by doing so they could meet more pilgrims. Most of the Santiago pilgrims walk about twenty kilometers (about ten miles) a day. Given the uniformity of distance, pilgrims usually see the same people throughout their trek. Hospitaleros, on the other hand, stay in one place, so they meet different people every day. Serving as a hospitalero, therefore, is a more efficient way to interact with more pilgrims.

Over the course of a month-long journey, many pilgrims may feel ill or injure themselves. Some may misjudge the distance of their day's walk and run out of water in the mountains. When such incidents happen, they are reliant on others for help; perhaps a fellow-pilgrim who offers them water, or a hospitalero who happens to be a physician and can give medical treatment. Pilgrims consider these interactions to be the most valuable experiences they have on their journeys, ones which often trigger psychological growth or a change in values.

A Japanese pilgrim learned about the Camino de Santiago pilgrimage by reading Shirley MacLaine's *The Camino: A Journey of the Spirit*. She quit her job so that she could walk the pilgrimage route and examine her inner self with nothing else on her schedule to worry about. In the final chapter of her journal of her trip she didn't even mention the cathedral or Saint James. To her, the Camino de Santiago pilgrimage was "a trip full of nature, wind, water, fire and soil." She wrote that her days of walking, eating, and sleeping were simple and "made it easy for me to focus on my latent hopes and talents." She felt that the people she met along the way were there to teach her something (Singul, 2008).

As you can see, for many people, the objective is not reaching the Cathedral of Santiago de Compostela. For modern-day pilgrims the experiences along the way are important. The log of another Japanese woman who made the pilgrimage describes the end of her journey as anticlimactic. "After coming so far and making it to the goal, I felt not even a twinge of excitement" (Odajima 2008).

The deification of the Camino

Mennonite theologian Arthur P. Boers states that the route embodies a unique set of values based on trust and cooperation that is separate from the Catholic faith. His theory is that sharing meals, lodging, and intimate conversations with people you've just met are the modern characteristics of the Camino de Santiago pilgrimage.

Boers recounts the story of a female pilgrim he was with when he injured his foot. The two of them were walking together at first, but his pace slowed after the injury, and the woman went on ahead, reluctant to take on the job of looking after him. She had a change of heart, however, and walked back to find Boers. She took him to a hospital and stayed with him while he was being treated.

Boers says that as this sort of thing happens frequently, people tend to anthropomorphize or deify the route. When hearing about such an experience, they say, "Well, that's the Camino," convinced that it is the place itself that makes it happen. It is perhaps the number of these experiences —which rarely happen in daily life—that make the Santiago pilgrimage route so special and unique (Boers 2007).

According to a woman who is part of a Camino de Santiago pilgrim group in Japan, very few of the group's members are Catholic and there is little if any sense of "devoting oneself to Saint James." They refer to the route by its Spanish name of El Camino, and say they have "Camino faith." When you think about it, if the emphasis on modern pilgrimages is interpersonal experiences, "Camino faith" accurately describes the bond that forms among pilgrims and the process of the pilgrimage that facilitates that bond.

The Cathedral of Santiago de Compostela as "a rule of the game"

In a secular society, Saint James and his holy relics have meaning and worth only for devout believers. The anthropomorphizing and deification of the pilgrimage, as well as terms like "Camino faith" indicate that the objective of the pilgrimage is shifting away from a vertical faith with believers below and God and Saint James above, and toward a horizontal relationship in which the pilgrims are bonded together as a community.

Anthropologist Doi Kiyomi sees the Cathedral of Santiago de Compostela as "a rule of the game" (Hoshino et al 2012). It can no longer be said that arrival at the Cathedral of Santiago de Compostela to pray before the holy relics of Saint James is the essential motivation for modern-day pilgrims, as it was for pilgrims in the past. Without the goal of reaching the cathedral, however, those setting off independently to wander the more than eight hundred kilometers (about five hundred miles) of the Camino de Santiago would no longer be "pilgrims," but simply "trekkers." So, the only irrevocable rule of the pilgrimage is to head west until one reaches the cathedral. With this common goal, travelers are "pilgrims," undertaking a "pilgrimage." Saint James could be considered to have become a kind of symbol of the communication between pilgrims and their community.

The pilgrimage experience: process as objective

The Camino de Santiago pilgrimage route is not the only one that is being rediscovered and restructured. Brittany in France has the Tro Breizh route that pilgrims follow to pay homage to saints in their birthplaces. The route goes through seven different cities, and was revived as a walking pilgrimage at the end of the twentieth century.

Then there is the island monastery of Mont-Saint-Michel, also in France. Most tourists travel there by bus; it can be done as a day trip from Paris. Mont-Saint-Michel and its Bay was registered as a UNESCO Cultural World Heritage site in 1979, and in 1998 the site was also included as part of the World Heritage designation given to Routes of Santiago de Compostela in France. As a result, more and more pilgrims are visiting it on their way to Santiago. Mont-Saint-Michel is famous because the water surrounding it recedes completely when the tide is out. Although easily accessible by bridge at any time of day, there are tours that escort pilgrims on foot across the muddy flats of the bay to the monastery. The walk takes several hours and timing is of the essence, but pilgrims want to do it the way it was done in the Middle Ages.

In Japan, too, interest in walking pilgrimages is growing. The Shikoku Pilgrimage to the eighty-eight temples on the island of Shikoku comes to mind first. Others include walking tours from Tokyo to Mount Fuji and the Kumano Kodo pilgrimage routes on the Kii Peninsula in western Honshu.

Hoshino Eiki, a leading researcher on pilgrimages, says that the walking itself has become the purpose of making the walking pilgrimage in Shikoku. Just like the Camino de Santiago, the process of the Shikoku Pilgrimage has become the main focus. Pilgrims have broken away from the traditional religious reasons for making the pilgrimage. Hoshino tells the story of a guide for a bus tour of the temples on the Shikoku Pilgrimage route. In the course of the guide's work, she would see pilgrims on foot. She finally decided that a bus could not offer an authentic pilgrimage, so she set off on her own walking pilgrimage. The situation is the same on the Camino de Santiago pilgrimage route, with walkers frequently calling bus passengers and cyclists "false" pilgrims (Hoshino 2001).

A religious pilgrimage is, by definition, a trip to pray before sacred relics. The method of transportation used to get there is not important. People take cars and buses as a way to keep the cost of a pilgrimage down. Today, however, the lure of the holy relics waiting at the goal has waned. The goal of the pilgrimage and the method of the pilgrimage no longer match up. We have a situation where pilgrims without religious belief have come to attach importance to the process of walking to a religious site; and where pilgrims with religious belief, who simply want to pray before sacred relics, may choose a bus or a car as the most expeditious way to arrive at their goal.

Hoshino notes how pilgrimages with the emphasis on process can be interpreted as religious. The majority of modern pilgrims on the Shikoku Pilgrimage do not have traditional faith in Shingon Buddhism and its founder Kukai, with whom the pilgrimage sites are associated. By walking, however, they feel as though they are immersed in a different world, have had their spirit renewed, and been "given life." Hoshino avers that this sort of experience and spiritual realization is what is usually referred to as a religious experience, whether or not the person involved recognizes it as such.

The interpersonal exchanges between pilgrims focusing on process can be seen in many different places: pilgrimage blogs, Internet bulletin boards, video-sharing sites, information-sharing meet-ups among pilgrimage association members, and more. The emotional investment pilgrims have in the countless relationships formed on the extensive paths of the Santiago and Shikoku pilgrimages is evident.

When pilgrims tell the story of their own personal pilgrimages, however, what stands out is the similarity rather than the diversity of the episodes. Hoshino documents a shared series of spiritual realizations as well as a uniform appreciation for a simple lifestyle, gratitude for food and water, and a willingness to carry out and be recipients of acts of kindness. It is easy to see a pattern in pilgrims' stories of how they set out on a journey of their own free will, with no religious goal in mind, and how they discovered the value of exchange with people they met along the way.

Episodes on the pilgrimage route

Before they set out, modern-day pilgrims see films, read novels, and browse articles on the Internet. Based on the information they gather, they build up a picture of an authentic pilgrimage and the sorts of interpersonal experiences they need to have in order to achieve it. The pilgrims then seem to actively choose and emphatically convey experiences that match their picture, as seen in the following examples of pilgrims' own experiences:

> On my way down from the O Cebreiro mountain pass, I stopped in a small village (I can't remember its name). There was a light rain, and an elderly woman came up to me holding a plate of what looked like crepes stacked about five centimeters [two inches] high. "Help yourself," she said. I took a crepe and so did the two men I was with—one from Brazil and the other from Korea—and the woman shook salt over them. The instant we put them in our mouths, she said, "That'll be fifty cents." That's a pushy way to make a sale, I thought, but it was only fifty cents and it seemed worth her trouble. She had what looked to be about twenty crepes. At fifty cents each she'd make ten euros. It seemed like an easy way to make some cash, but I didn't begrudge the old woman the money to enjoy what was left of her life (Singul 2008).

This crepe vendor is famous on the Camino de Santiago pilgrimage route, and she is a frequent topic of discussion among pilgrims. Stories about her tend to be negative, as evident in the word "pushy." The author of one guidebook wrote that she felt "duped" (Nakatani 2004). The criticism seems overly harsh for an old woman who has scammed the pilgrim out of less than a dollar.

I met the elderly crepe vendor myself during a survey I was conducting in 2008. When I passed through the village of Fonfria in the drizzling rain, she burst out from the shadows of a humble dwelling with a big smile saying, "Tired pilgrim, help yourself to a crepe." This woman matched an image travelers are looking for—a pious farmer's wife in a lonely hamlet, who acts out of kindness to pilgrims. Deceived by their own preconceptions, most pilgrims accept the crepe without question. When they find out the woman is there to make money, they become angry. Why? Because they realize that the woman is making money by deliberately playing on their arbitrary preconceptions.

Father José Maria, a priest who runs an albergue in the village of San Juan de Ortega, is the opposite of the crepe vendor. The priest is known for the garlic soup he makes for pilgrims who stay with him. Here is a description of him from the same guidebook.

> Father José, who is serving *sopa de ajo* (garlic soup), has been making it for pilgrims every day for the past half century. He pours out the soup into enamel cups that appear to have seen long years of service. Since the soup contains bread, it is filling. After the pilgrims finish it, Father José gives them each a warm handshake. Father José, I hope you are healthy for many more years to come.
>
> You can only get this soup if you attend mass, so I recommend that you do!

This priest appears in many written accounts of Camino de Santiago pilgrimages, as well as in guidebooks. In contrast to the crepe vendor, Father José is usually referred to with affection.

As mentioned in the above excerpt, however, the priest's soup is only given to those who attend mass. At mass, of course, an offering will be collected, and I imagine that most pilgrims will put more than fifty cents into the plate as it comes around. Someone with a cynical viewpoint might say Father José is doing better business than the crepe vendor.

Father José Maria is also mentioned in Shirley MacLaine's book. During her pilgrimage, she was followed around by paparazzi. The actress was victimized in a multitude of ways including having a shower curtain pushed aside so a photographer could get shots of her while naked. Just before she reached San Juan de Ortega, the home of Father José, the mobs of paparazzi mysteriously disappeared. Here is the episode in MacLaine's words.

Then I came into San Juan de Ortega and realized why the press had seemed to dissipate along the Camino.

There were two hundred of them waiting for me at the church. Ali and Carlos were waiting there too. Carlos came to meet me and told me that the priest had offered the journalists an interview with me in return for a donation to his church. I told Carlos to tell them I didn't think it was fair. He readily accommodated and told them off, including the priest.

The priest offered me garlic soup, which I refused and continued on my way.

In the end, Father José and the crepe vendor appear to have the same motives. The reason why most pilgrims reacted favorably to the priest, however, was because he was playing a certain role—priest of a church along the route overflowing with goodness. Collecting money in the form of a church offering was a good match for the experiences pilgrims were looking for. For those who rarely went to mass or who were not members of the Catholic Church, giving an offering during a worship service added to the specialness of the pilgrimage. Nonreligious pilgrims got exactly what they wanted on the stage prepared for them by the priest, and were quick to praise him for it.

Patterns of interpersonal experiences

Modern nonbeliever pilgrims on the Camino de Santiago route appear to be taking the journey in a form that is removed from the framework of Catholic traditions and that accords with their own preferences. The free will they assume they are exercising, however, is actually highly—if not consciously—prescribed and far from unique.

Anthropologist Kadota Takehisa calls the modern Shikoku Pilgrimage a "shallow religious experience." By "shallow" he does not mean that the experience is superficial or inferior to an authentic religious experience. For example, in a survey he made of the members of a bus tour to Shikoku, he observed that all participants had their own personal (but, in fact, common) experiences, which they talked about with each other and from which they derived a great deal of satisfaction. He came to the conclusion that being satisfied with a "good-enough religious experience," as opposed to one that is mystical, is a sign of the wholesomeness of today's pilgrims (Kadota 2013).

This author holds the same opinion. I have no intention of criticizing modern Camino de Santiago pilgrims for putting emphasis on personal interactions and exchanges. After spending a great deal of time and money to go on this pilgrimage, pilgrims do not talk about the magnificence of the Cathedral of Santiago de Compostela or personal religious conversion. They talk about sharing water and eating with others, what would appear to be minor experiences, but which to them are priceless. But it should also be emphasized that these experiences can, in theory, be had almost anywhere.

Camino de Santiago pilgrims talk repeatedly about the relationships and interactions they experience along the route because, in reality, these exchanges have become unusual in modern society. Secularization and privatization mean that people can no longer assume that they share a religious story or its values with most of society. And this in turn means that people don't expect to be accepted unconditionally or helped when in need. It has become rare for anyone to have a stable sense of belonging to a place or a group, or to have communal attitudes. This is why the connections and experiences gained on a pilgrimage route make such a vivid impression.

While a traditional Catholic believer takes a pilgrimage to offer a fervent prayer before a holy relic, nonreligious pilgrims want experiences based on interpersonal exchange. If exchange between a human and a supreme being or saint offers a vertical and transcendental experience, secular pilgrims are in search of horizontal experiences between themselves and other humans. If the efforts of the secular pilgrim result in the interpersonal exchange they are hoping for, it will most likely lead to spiritual realizations and new ways of thinking.

Just because tourism has been mixed into pilgrimages doesn't mean that pilgrimages have less depth. The journey of a nonbeliever is no less authentic than that of a believer. We can say, however, that the mix of tourism and religion has resulted in new patterns of experiences.

Pilgrims gain satisfaction from their journeys even if they do not have a great knowledge of religion or fervent faith. It is important to realize that pilgrimages can no longer be discussed within a framework of whether or not the journey is religious or secular. Secular pilgrims have had new experiences during the Camino de Santiago pilgrimage, but these have only been gained by intentionally extending the process of getting there and by actively connecting with people on the way. This does not mean that religion has been lost, rather that it is expanding beyond its traditional framework and taking on a new shape.

World Heritage Sites and Holy Places: Discriminating between Religious Cultures

Chapter 3

In this chapter, we will be looking at nonreligious authorities and systems and considering their influence on traditional religious culture, in particular, that of the World Heritage organization run by the United Nations Educational, Scientific and Cultural Organization (UNESCO). When UNESCO, governments, and other outside organizations judge holy sites and religions, what is considered valuable and what is not? What is behind such values? Answers to these questions should provide clues as to how religion is positioned in a secular society.

The World Heritage system has an enormous influence, especially in Japan. Designation as a World Heritage site results in publicity and a jump in tourism. There is always a long list of candidates waiting for consideration. As various places undertake promotional activities to boost their chances of acceptance onto the World Heritage List, we can see how some sites edit their religious significance for secular consumption. Let us use the World Heritage system, with its enormous appeal, to take a critical look at how religious culture functions in a secular society, with a particular focus on religion and tourism.

The World Heritage system and religious culture

The Convention Concerning the Protection of the World Cultural and Natural Heritage (adopted in 1972, effective as of 1975) is a system operated by UNESCO. Japan ratified the convention in 1992, and in the following year, four Japanese sites were registered: Buddhist Monuments in the Horyu-ji Area and Himeji Castle were designated as cultural heritage sites; and the primeval forest of Shirakami Sanchi in Aomori and

Yakushima Island off Kyushu were designated as natural heritage sites. In the following years, more cultural sites were designated:

Historic Monuments of Ancient Kyoto (1994)
Historic Villages of Shirakawa-go and Gokayama (1995)
Hiroshima Peace Memorial (1996)
Itsukushima Shinto Shrine (1996)
Historic Monuments of Ancient Nara (1998)
Shrines and Temples of Nikko (1999)
Gusuku Sites and Related Properties of the Kingdom of Ryukyu (2000)
Sacred Sites and Pilgrimage Routes in the Kii Mountain Range (2004)
Iwami Ginzan Silver Mine and its Cultural Landscape (2007)
Hiraizumi—Temples, Gardens and Archaeological Sites Representing the Buddhist Pure Land (2011)
Fujisan, sacred place and source of artistic inspiration (2013)
Tomioka Silk Mill and Related Sites (2014)
Sites of Japan's Meiji Industrial Revolution: Iron and Steel, Shipbuilding and Coal Mining (2015)
The Architectural Work of Le Corbusier, an Outstanding Contribution to the Modern Movement (2016)
The Sacred Island of Okinoshima and Associated Sites in the Munakata Region (2017)
Hidden Christian Sites in the Nagasaki and Amakusa Region (2018)

Looking over this list, we can see that almost all of these places were well-known even before they were labeled World Heritage sites. Nikko and Kyoto are standard tourist attractions in Japan. The Hiroshima Peace Memorial features in the Japanese school curriculum and is often chosen for school trips.

UNESCO states that a place must meet at least one of the following criteria in order to be registered as a World Heritage site. (Conditions for natural heritage sites have been left out.)

(i)   represent a masterpiece of human creative genius;
(ii) exhibit an important interchange of human values, over a span

of time or within a cultural area of the world, on developments in architecture or technology, monumental arts, town-planning or landscape design;

(iii) bear a unique or at least exceptional testimony to a cultural tradition or to a civilization which is living or which has disappeared;

(iv) be an outstanding example of a type of building, architectural or technological ensemble or landscape which illustrates (a) significant stage(s) in human history;

(v) be an outstanding example of a traditional human settlement, land-use, or sea-use which is representative of a culture (or cultures), or human interaction with the environment especially when it has become vulnerable under the impact of irreversible change;

(vi) be directly or tangibly associated with events or living traditions, with ideas, or with beliefs, with artistic and literary works of outstanding universal significance. (The Committee considers that this criterion should preferably be used in conjunction with other criteria.)

An issue touched on in chapter 1, and which is evident in these conditions, is that authenticity and integrity are important points when selecting a cultural World Heritage site. This is why the reproduction of Shurijo Castle (see chapter 1) was not registered but the site of the original castle was. The World Heritage system strives to physically preserve sites that have been evaluated historically and academically as authentic. Because of this, structures in Japan that are chosen, by definition, already have established reputations. Only criterion (vi) includes nonmaterial things, living traditions, ideas, and beliefs. As indicated in parentheses, however, this condition "should preferably be used in conjunction with other criteria."

The concept of the cultural landscape

The number of World Heritage listings continues to grow, despite the fact that fewer candidates have established values of historical or archaeological authenticity or integrity. One reason for this is the introduction in

1992 of the "cultural landscape" concept.

Cultural landscapes are given the following definition by World Heritage: "Combined works of nature and humankind, they express a long and intimate relationship between peoples and their natural environment." World Heritage divides cultural landscapes into three categories, which can be paraphrased as follows:

(1) The clearly defined landscape designed and created intentionally by man. This embraces garden and parkland landscapes constructed for aesthetic reasons which are often (but not always) associated with religious or other monumental buildings and ensembles.

(2) The organically evolved landscape resulting from an initial social economic, administrative, and/or religious imperative. This landscape has developed its present form by association with and in response to its natural environment.

(3) Associative cultural landscapes: where the interaction between people and the landscape is strongly linked to ideas or beliefs.

The first category refers to places of scenic beauty and historical sites. This is not much different from the original World Heritage standpoint of choosing cultural assets from a material point of view. The second and third categories, on the other hand, emphasize human interaction with the environment, including interactions that continue to the present day. The second category refers to landscapes like terraced rice fields, which are more tangible and material, while the third type of cultural landscape has more of a spiritual and intangible nature, that finds its expression through religion and art.

With the addition of the "cultural landscapes" category to World Heritage sites, the position of religion—which had up to that point consisted of material things—has expanded somewhat. At the very least, this category makes it easier to consider religion not just in terms of vestiges of the past, but also as it is practiced to the present day. In the case of the Camino de Santiago pilgrimage described in chapter 2, the pilgrimage path itself is registered as a World Heritage site, although emphasis is placed on the shrines, temples and churches that remain along the route, such as the Burgos Cathedral, itself a World Heritage site, as well as the Eunate Church and other old Romanesque houses of worship.

The Sacred Sites and Pilgrimage Routes in the Kii Mountain Range is similar to the World Heritage–designated Routes of Santiago de Compostela. The former includes shrines in the prefectures of Nara, Mie, and Wakayama, including the three Kumano Sanzan shrines, Kinpusenji Temple, and Kongobuji Temple. The site is home to a total of four structures that the Japanese government has designated as national treasures and more than twenty that it has designated important cultural properties.

A problem crops up, however, when considering religion and World Heritage sites. Promoting places devoted to living religions is not easy in countries like Japan where church and state are separate. In Japan, individual prefectures (similar to states or counties) are usually in charge of promotional activities, and in the final stage of the domestic application process, the national government recommends a site to UNESCO. Since religion tends to be linked to local culture and history, it is easy to use a site's value as a local symbol and its overall allure as constituent elements required of a World Heritage site. However, since the government is forbidden to have links to a particular religion, it must exercise caution. Because of this situation, religious culture tends to be emphasized in terms of tradition and customs rather than as an active institution.

Mount Fuji as a cultural landscape

Let us look at some World Heritage sites based on their criteria for designation as cultural landscapes, as outlined in the previous section. Note how their suitability has been analyzed and processed to make sure religion does not come into conflict with the World Heritage system.

First, let's take the case of Mount Fuji, which was registered as a World Heritage site in 2013. Yamanashi and Shizuoka prefectural governments were the main driving forces behind efforts to get the iconic mountain recognized, and it took twenty years. Initial attempts to have Mount Fuji registered as a natural World Heritage site were unsuccessful; success came when the mountain was put forward as a cultural site in which religion has played a major role.

The initial application attempts had several problems. Mount Fuji is covered with trash thrown away by climbers, and the mountain type is not unique. Mount Kilimanjaro had already been registered as a strato-volcano, and its natural environment is much better preserved. For these reasons, Mount Fuji was twice eliminated from consideration at the domestic selection stage. Then the decision was made to change gears and attempt to have it registered as a cultural asset, focusing on the key concept of "historical religious faith."

The recommendation submitted to UNESCO claimed that Mount Fuji satisfied three of the World Heritage selection criteria (see pp. 80–81). First, "Mount Fuji faith" was an example of a cultural tradition (criterion iii). Second, it was an outstanding cultural landscape recognized around the world (criterion iv), and third, it had a connection to works of art (criterion vi). In the end, UNESCO recognized criterion iii and criterion vi. In criterion iii the term *religious faith* was used in the recommendation, not to describe a religion still in practice, but one from the past as expressed through material things, in this case the miniature replicas of Mount Fuji, described below, that are found today in the precincts of Tokyo temples and which date from an era when there was a widespread faith centering on Mount Fuji. For criterion vi, Mount Fuji's frequent appearance in ukiyo-e woodblock prints of the Edo era (1603–1868), and the fame of this genre overseas, had given the mountain universal value.

Let us look more closely at the "historical religious faith" that was claimed as an example of something that bore "exceptional testimony to a cultural tradition," as stated in UNESCO's criterion iii.

From ancient times, Mount Fuji was a site of mountain veneration, a place associated with mountain asceticism (Shugendo). In the early Edo era, a mountain ascetic named Kakugyo (1541–1646) created a unique doctrine of Mount Fuji faith that differed from the traditional mountaineering asceticism and training known as Shugendo. His ideas and practices were carried on and further developed by Jikigyo Miroku (1671–1733), who financed the spread of the religion himself. Jikigyo's final act was to fast to death on Eboshi Rock on the slope of Mount Fuji in order to bring salvation to all living beings. What Jikigyo taught became the core of Mount Fuji faith, and gave rise to pilgrimage organizations known as

Fujiko, which became explosively popular during the eighteenth and early nineteenth centuries among the Edo populace. These pilgrimage associations (*ko*), comprising groups of believers that visited and paid homage at temples, shrines, and sacred mountains such as Mount Fuji, supported the vibrant pilgrimage culture of the time. The phrase "808 ko in the 808 districts of Edo" describes the widespread practice of worshipers making trips from Edo to the mountain and climbing it as a sign of devotion.

At this time in Japan's history, however, not many believers could afford an annual trip to the top of Mount Fuji, so shrines and temples, mainly in the Tokyo area, constructed miniature replicas of the famous peak, called *fujizuka*. The miniatures were sometimes made using pieces of lava carried from Mount Fuji. Most fujizuka are only four to ten meters (thirteen to thirty feet) high, but are modeled on the climbing path from the first stage to the peak and include important landmarks, such as Eboshi Rock and Hitoana, a cave where Kakugyo spent time as an ascetic.

Members of Fujiko would climb the miniature replicas on the opening day of the Fuji climbing season in July, in the belief that the spiritual effects would be the same as if they had climbed the real mountain. Most fujizuka in Tokyo were destroyed during World War II air raids, but there are some that remain in good condition today, such as those at Onoterusaki Shrine in Shitaya (which is designated as an important cultural property), Teppozuinari Shrine in Hatchobori, and Hatonomori Hachiman Shrine in Sendagaya. A few shrines and temples with fujizuka still celebrate the opening of the climbing season each year (Plate 6).

The heyday of Mount Fuji faith ended with the Meiji Revolution in 1868, when Japan's new government refused to officially recognize Fujiko. Fujiko remains today as a sect of the animistic Shinto religion, but it is not particularly active. After World War II, climbing Mount Fuji became mainly a leisure activity, leaving little behind of traditional Fujiko activities.

This was the historical background for promoting Mount Fuji as a cultural World Heritage site and the reason why the mountain was presented not as a natural heritage site, but as a "sacred mountain." In other words, the strategy behind the World Heritage application was not to emphasize leisure or tourism, but to give religious meaning to Mount Fuji. A draft of the proposal made to UNESCO in 2011 said "the essence of the cultural tradition of Mount Fuji" had been handed down to the present day, and that climbing the peak today embodied "values that are different from modern-day alpinism."

In 2011, Fuji Yoshida Station on the Fujikyuko railway line was renamed Mount Fuji Station. To emphasize Mount Fuji as an object of worship, an enormous *torii* gate was built at the station entrance. This gate is based on the one at Fujisan Hongu Sengen Shrine, the traditional starting point for climbing Mount Fuji. There are also plans to reconstruct the district next to the station, where *oshi*, guides and assistants for pilgrims to Mount Fuji, lived during the Edo era.

This was how the Japanese government officials behind the movement to get Mount Fuji registered as a World Heritage site handled a faith that had worshiped the mountain for hundreds of years or longer. In other words, the argument was made that this was a faith whose existence had been recorded in historical documents, and which had tangible physical evidence.

In addition, however, World Heritage required proof of continuing belief in Mount Fuji as a sacred mountain. As mentioned above, the Japanese government claimed that when the mountain is climbed—even today—it is according to values that are different from run-of-the-mill mountain climbing for sport.

It cannot be denied that people do make the ascent for the purpose of gaining energy or being able to "find" themselves, and Mount Fuji is often referred to as a "power spot." There are even tours that invite people to climb Mount Fuji and practice yoga while watching the sun rise. It could be said, however, that the force behind the current Mount Fuji climbing boom is not based on the beliefs of Fujiko begun by Jikigyo but is more akin to the motivation of modern Camino de Santiago pilgrims. The World Heritage site notion of choosing cultural assets from a material point of view overlooks any possible religious inspiration felt by present-day mountaineers. In other words, there is an enormous gap between the government's reconsideration of a historical religion in order to get Mount Fuji designated as a World Heritage site and the actual religious feeling of people who climb the mountain today. This distance between public claims and individual experience is even clearer in our next case, that of the Kumano Kodo pilgrimage routes.

The Kumano Kodo pilgrimage routes as "cultural landscape"

The Sacred Sites and Pilgrimage Routes in the Kii Mountain Range was registered as a cultural World Heritage site in 2004 due to the efforts of governments in three prefectures: Mie, Nara, and Wakayama. Among the shrines included are Kumano Hongu, Kumano Hayatama, and Kumano Nachi, all in the south of the Kii Peninsula and said to have been built during the Nara period (710–794). Nobles and commoners alike paid visits to these shrines between the twelfth and the sixteenth centuries.

Amada Akinori, a scholar of the Kumano Kodo pilgrimage routes of the Kii Mountain Range, has noticed a change in the attitudes of the people who live in the area since the World Heritage designation. He gives the example of a unique group of female guides that has been formed. The women have modeled themselves on twelfth-century Kumano nuns who helped spread the Kumano faith by explaining the meanings of the paintings that illustrated it. The modern-day guides are basically volunteers, but they participate in study groups. The result of their efforts, they say, is that they have discovered how special the sights are that they see every day. They do not consider themselves tools of religion. Their job, they say, is to convey "something special" about Kumano that tourism alone cannot communicate (Amada 2012).

Through the process of obtaining the World Heritage site label, forgotten religious resources have been dug up and the local people identify more strongly with the area and have nurtured a sense of community. As they have become aware of the viewpoint of outsiders, they have begun to see aspects of their ordinary lives as something extraordinary and a source of spirituality.

This shift in attitude resonates with some visitors to Kumano. Foreign tourists who read the *Michelin Green Guide to Japan* will see that the book gives three stars to the Kumano Kodo pilgrimage routes, Nachinotaki Falls, Daimonzaka Hill (Plate 7), and the three mountains of Kumano.

Thanks to ratings like these, more people from overseas come to walk the pilgrimage routes. The "pilgrims" describe their experience as one of new spiritual awareness and realization of their own connection with nature, very similar to what Camino de Santiago pilgrims have to say. In other words, this is neither traditional religion nor simple sightseeing: these visitors simply feel the "something special" that their hosts wish to offer them.

Let us not forget, however, the enormous gap between the attitudes of the locals and those of the authorities who worked to achieve the World Heritage designation. Member of the local government, Oda Seitaro, bemoans the fact that, while the number of visitors to the area has increased dramatically, most of them "go home having been unable to see the forest for the trees."

According to Oda, one needs an enormous amount of knowledge about an infinite number of constituent elements in order to appreciate and understand this particular World Heritage site. Most of the visitors to Kumano may have a temporary religious experience from spending time in nature and seeing the beautiful scenery. From the viewpoint of those connected to the World Heritage system, however, this is misplaced excitement born of a lack of knowledge about the things they have seen (Oda 2010).

In many cases this lack of knowledge begets pseudo-religious stories and practices, which are then supported by cities and prefectures. Right next to Kumano Hongu Shrine is the Kumano Hongu Heritage Center, which was built in 2009 by Wakayama Prefecture and Tanabe City at a cost of over ¥800,000,000 (about US$7,000,000) to commemorate the fifth anniversary of the area's designation as a World Heritage site. The purpose of the center is to offer information on tourism in the Kumano Kodo area, and it accommodates the Wakayama World Heritage Center, Tanabe Tourism Bureau Hongu Office, Kumano Hongu Sightseeing Association, the Kumano Hongu Storyteller Group, and the nonprofit organization Health Lab in Kumano.

The Health Lab is trying to promote Kumano as a health resort so that the sightseeing boom spurred by its World Heritage designation will not be a passing fad. To this end, they have conjured up the notion of healing through walking the Kumano Kodo pilgrimage routes. The Health Lab website, www.kumano-de-kenko.com, introduces Oyunohara as a relaxing therapy spot. Oyunohara is the original site of the Hongu Grand Shrine, which stood on a sandbar at the confluence of three rivers —the Kumano, the Otonashi, and the Iwata—until it was washed away by a flood in 1889. Under the header "Oyunohara has an ideal feng shui landform!!" the website claims the spot retains its energy through the preservation of the forests, rivers, and ponds surrounding it.

The website cites as its source a basic survey of health promotion tourism at World Heritage sites by the Ministry of Land, Infrastructure, Transport and Tourism, and the Kinki District Transport Bureau, Wakayama Prefecture (2005). The source document includes descriptions such as "Oyunohara with its ideal feng shui landform seems to have the power of a holy place" and "The restoration of Oyunohara is an important element of regional recovery." The study draws the following conclusion:

> *Prayer* and *healing* represent religion and medicine, which are essentially the same. The fusion of the two is important for the fundamental therapy of physical and mental ailments of modern people. This combination of prayer and healing makes it possible to encourage visitors to Kumano shrines to stay longer for therapeutic purposes.

This sounds like a guidebook for a power spot. It is unusual for an official document to use such religious-sounding expressions. The same document also describes the possibility of a program to train unemployed young people for occupations in tree planting, thinning, and road maintenance. This author is not criticizing pseudo practices and stories as infringing on the separation of religion and state. The greater issue is that the cultural heritage and traditions of Kumano are being adapted to modern society for the sake of promoting tourism. Religious theories do not always agree with modern values or ethics. More often than not, they do the opposite. Picking out and altering parts of religion to make them more palatable goes against the true purpose of transmitting history and culture.

Secularization converging with religious culture

The Mount Omine route is the most demanding of the Kumano Kodo pilgrimage routes, and it has sparked a different debate. Omine has a long history of the mountaineering asceticism and training known as Shugendo. Its followers, called *yamabushi*, still train by walking the Omine-okugake trail along high mountain ridges.

Mount Sanjogatake is the site of Ominesanji Temple, the most important center for Shugendo. Here though there is an issue: according to religious tradition, women are not allowed anywhere on the mountain. The area is part of a national park, however, and considered of value for all humankind as a cultural World Heritage site. As such, some people feel that women should be allowed to go there.

This is one typical way in which religious values conflict with modern values. The Kumano Kodo pilgrimage routes have been given World Heritage status because the traditions are deeply rooted and have continued for so long. Once a sacred site draws attention to itself in this way, however, there can be friction between religious culture and secular values.

There is, in fact, another holy Japanese World Heritage site that forbids women, the Sacred Island of Okinoshima and Associated Sites in the Munakata Region. Since ancient times, this uninhabited island in the Genkai Sea, near Fukuoka in Kyushu, has been a strategic point for marine traffic from the Asian continent. At the same time, the entire island is an object of worship and women are forbidden to step foot on it. Previously, men were only allowed once a year, on May 27, for a festival to commemorate the 1905 Naval Battle of the Sea of Japan during the Russo-Japanese War. For this annual occasion, two hundred men were chosen by lottery to visit the island. This event, however, was banned by Munakata Taisha Shrine following World Heritage registration in 2017.

A similar example in another country is Mount Athos in Greece, which was registered as a World Heritage site in 1988. Monks began living on the mountain during the seventh century. Today about 1,400 monks lead celibate lives on Mount Athos. The land is within the borders of Greece, but the monks are self-governing. Visitors, therefore, are required to go through immigration procedures, and their numbers are strictly regulated. Priority is given to visits by Orthodox believers, and entrance is forbidden to women and children.

The historical sacred space Sefa-utaki

Tourism researcher Kadota Takehisa has debated how religious culture has been pulled apart and compartmentalized by World Heritage site designations, using as his example Sefa-utaki in Okinawa (Kadota 2013). As mentioned in chapter 1, the word *utaki* means a sacred place for special rituals and ceremonies according to traditional Ryukyuan beliefs. The most sacred of these places is Sefa-utaki (Plate 8), whose high priestess has the title Kikoe Okimi.

In 2000, Sefa-utaki was registered as a World Heritage site as a part of the Gusuku Sites and Related Properties of the Kingdom of Ryukyu. According to Kadota, this designation caused a division in the religious culture of Sefa-utaki. Historically the Okinawan religion had two main components: the first consisting of a pilgrimage known as Agari Umaai along with other public celebrations; the second consisting of private shamanic activities conducted by shamans known as *yuta*, who make

Sefa-utaki in Okinawa.

petitions on behalf of believers, tell fortunes, and so on. When Sefa-utaki was registered as a World Heritage site, its public practices, such as the Agari Umaai pilgrimage were recognized, but not the private religious practices carried out by the yuta shamans. Moreover, because the newly designated Heritage site was surrounded by trees, the incense-burning rituals frequently carried out by the yuta were banned. In other words, the existence of the yuta, who carry on the practices of traditional Ryukyuan religious culture, is now considered a risk to this officially designated sacred spot.

Although many sacred places would love to be designated as World Heritage sites, the emphasis on material things gets in the way of religious practice, of which the shamans in the previous paragraph are a good example. When considering a place for World Heritage designation, even religious culture is judged by secular institutions looking for a retail value. The fate of these places lies in whether they are considered business or tourism assets.

The application for World Heritage status for Okinoshima

In 2017, the Sacred Island of Okinoshima and Associated Sites in the Munakata Region was designated as a World Heritage site, and this is a good example of how political tactics concerning cultural properties can influence religious practices. When Japan first applied for designation, the International Council on Monuments and Sites (ICOMOS), the advisory organization for UNESCO, recommended that only part of the candidate group was suitable for designation. When the World Heritage Committee convened in Poland, however, this recommendation was ignored and all of the assets were registered.

Let's look at the process. Here is a list of the assets that the Japan side applied for, which includes the three branches of the Munakata Taisha Shrine.

1. Okitsu-miya Munakata Taisha Shrine (Okinoshima Island and its three reefs, Koyajima, Mikadobashira, and Tenguiwa. Women are prohibited; men are also usually prohibited.)
2. Area for offering prayers at Okitsu-miya Yohaisho worship hall,

Munakata Taisha Shrine (Oshima Island, just under thirty minutes by ferry from the main Kyushu island)

3. Nakatsu-miya Munakata Taisha Shrine (Oshima Island)
4. Hetsu-miya Munakata Taisha Shrine (Kyushu main island)
5. Shimbaru-Nuyama Mounded Tomb Group (Kyushu main island)

In ancient days, Okinoshima was an important island in terms of maritime traffic between Japan and the Asian continent and was the site of major rituals to pray for safe ocean voyages. Many artifacts have been discovered to back this up, such as bronze mirrors, iron swords, and other weapons. Not only that, but they were not buried under layers of soil, but found right out in the open. Eighty thousand items have been designated as national treasures in Japan. In their application for World Heritage status the Japan side labeled Okinoshima as "Island of the Gods." The related sites on Okinoshima, Oshima, and Kyushu, homes to the Munakata Taisha shrines enshrining three goddesses, as well as the Shimbaru-Nuyama tombs of the Munakata clan, ancient rulers of the region, were also added.

It was the job of ICOMOS to study and evaluate the applications from an academic perspective. ICOMOS works for the protection and preservation of cultural assets, and has members who are specialists in many fields, including construction, preservation studies, archaeology, art history, and museology. ICOMOS concluded that only item (1), Okinoshima and its three reefs, was worth being registered. One of the reservations that ICOMOS had about this application for World Heritage status was whether Munakata Taisha Shrine had actually continued to practice the Okinoshima faith over the centuries. The relics found on Okinoshima proved that the faith had been practiced from the fourth to the ninth century. There was no scientific proof that Munakata Taisha had carried on the faith after that.

The Japan side argued that Munakata was mentioned as the name of a shrine in the ancient Japanese history books, the Chronicles of Japan (*Nihon shoki*) and Records of Ancient Matters (*Kojiki*). ICOMOS, however, noted that only the name was in these documents. There was no mention of the location. The Okinoshima faith is known to have predated the

Munakata Taisha shrines on Kyushu, Okinoshima and Oshima, and there was no proof that the faith had been continued in these places. In addition, the organization said, the Shimbaru-Nuyama burial mounds were ruins that did not merit more than local or national attention. Universal value is one of the conditions for World Heritage designation.

Furthermore, ICOMOS expressed doubts about the taboos related to Okinoshima. Women are forbidden from landing on the island, and men are restricted as well. When clerics go to the island, all purifications are conducted completely in the nude. No one is ever allowed to talk about what they see or hear there, nor can any plant or stone be removed from the island.

According to ICOMOS, these taboos were never mentioned before the seventeenth century; in other words, they were not that old. They also asserted that rituals and religious practices carried out on Okinoshima and at Munakata Taisha Shrine had only been revived in recent years, meaning that practices carried out in the past had been reinterpreted, and were not being passed on continuously and unchanged.

When the World Heritage committee convened in Poland, however, the ICOMOS recommendations were thrown out and all candidate assets were registered. This does not mean that academic doubts have been wiped away; it was more a matter of lobbying activities taking precedence. Indeed, the committee often rejects academic declarations for the sake of political and market principles.

The editing and transformation of religious culture: The Shikoku Pilgrimage

Cultural World Heritage sites are generally selected using criteria based on material items. Some candidate sites, however, try to compensate for obscure practices and a lack of material objects by developing new images for themselves. This trend is particularly noticeable among Tentative List candidates and candidates aiming for inclusion on the list.

Let's look at the campaign conducted by the council for promoting the Shikoku Pilgrimage route as a cultural World Heritage site (hereafter promotion council), which set itself the goal of making the Tentative List by 2016. This campaign aimed to have the eighty-eight temples and pil-

Pilgrims on foot traveling along the Shikoku Pilgrimage route.

grimage routes across 1,400 kilometers (870 miles) of the island of Shikoku designated in the same manner as the vast pilgrimage routes of the Camino de Santiago and the Kumano Kodo in the Kii Mountain Range.

The promotion council was configured from several groups. Of them, a group set up to "prove universal value" made an interesting report. To have the Shikoku Pilgrimage route recognized as a World Heritage site, they had to prove "outstanding universal value" and "exceptional significance" by means of material objects. After repeated discussions, however, they gave up on the attempt.

Some of the eighty-eight designated temples in Shikoku have material objects that could withstand examination by UNESCO. For example, Ishiteji Temple in Matsuyama, Ehime Prefecture, boasts the Niomon Gate, a Japanese national treasure. Two of its halls and a bell tower are designated by the government as important cultural properties. This temple also has a shrine with graffiti by Natsume Soseki and Masaoka Shiki, famous literary figures from the Meiji period (1868–1912). Many other temples, however, lost buildings to multiple fires during the Warring States period (1467–1568), making it difficult to produce material evidence for all the temples on the pilgrimage route. The promotion council therefore concluded that despite the number of remaining temples and cultural properties, these tangible assets were insufficient to prove the essential value of the entire Shikoku Pilgrimage route.

To overcome this lack of tangible items, the council looked for *intangible value* and came up with pilgrimages made on foot. The council defined walking pilgrims as the creators of the central value of the Shikoku Pilgrimage, claiming that "walking has been the basic form of the pilgrimage from early-modern to modern times." They said, "the physical act of walking, or physical ascetic training, gives pilgrims peace of mind, deepens their self-awareness, and fosters the religious oneness they feel with Kukai, the founder of Shingon Buddhism." This concept was proposed as the strategy for proving the pilgrimage path worthy of designation as a cultural World Heritage site. (Plate 9)

However, the claim that walking is the traditional and proper way of carrying out this pilgrimage is not historically correct. In the years following World War II, most pilgrims visited the temples by car or toured around in buses (Hoshino and Asakawa 2011). In the later years of the Showa period (1926–1989), pilgrims were seen only at the *fudasho*, the temple offices where travelers obtained slips of paper proving they had been there. It was not until after the 1990s that walkers began to increase in Shikoku, about the same time the Camino de Santiago pilgrimage (discussed in chapter 2) began to grow in popularity. It was right about the time that Japanese films and dramas came out with walking pilgrimages as their theme, and these had a strong influence on society.

Even prior to the pilgrimage boom of the 1990s, there were many Japanese works using the Shikoku Pilgrimage as a main motif. One example is *Suna no Utsuwa* [Castle of sand], originally a novel by mystery writer Matsumoto Seicho, published as a newspaper serial between 1960 and 1961, and later made into one film and five television dramas. In the story, one of the protagonists suffers from leprosy and is thrown out of his hometown due to prejudice and discrimination. He then goes on the Shikoku Pilgrimage in search of a place to die. The world of the pilgrimage is depicted as mystical and separate from the rest of society, governed by a religious order and its values.

The twenty-first century saw the making of the movie *Road 88: Deaiji, Shikoku e* [Road 88: Meet you in Shikoku, 2004], and the NHK television series *Walkers—Lost Adults* (2006). These both featured nonbelievers in Buddhism who were on the trek around Shikoku's eighty-eight temples for nonreligious reasons. As the titles suggest, a recurring theme was characters gaining awareness through exchange with people they met on the pilgrimage path, not religion. As we learned in chapter 2, books and films about Camino de Santiago pilgrims with non-Christian motives also flourished around this time, serving as motives for many to make the pilgrimage.

The Japanese productions above are works of imagination, and do not reflect all the realities of the Shikoku Pilgrimage. Still, we can see a shift in the image of the pilgrimage over the last half century, that is, transformation from a religious world isolated from ordinary life into a tourist destination people can easily visit.

A major difference between the Shikoku and Santiago pilgrimages is that in Shikoku, there are more walkers than there used to be, but their number is estimated at only several thousand. This is small compared to the three hundred thousand pilgrims the Camino de Santiago attracts every year from all over the world. Walking is not a central aspect of the Shikoku Pilgrimage, although this aspect is featured in many films and is emphasized by the council that promotes the pilgrimage.

Here the author wishes to reiterate the fact that this pilgrimage has been redefined as a walking pilgrimage in order to gain World Heritage designation, and walking is being presented as an intrinsic aspect of the traditional Shikoku Pilgrimage. This occurred when religious sites and activities that had long enjoyed a distinctive local presence were assessed against the international criteria of the cultural World Heritage system. The result has been the editing of religious culture—deciding what to spotlight and what to push into the background. Worthy of note is how a new value of the pilgrimage, hidden in its local context, has been uncovered and processed to fit the separate and distinct context of World Heritage. The material elements of the Shikoku Pilgrimage have receded into the background while the spotlight is placed on the religious experience and awareness gained through walking, in other words, a more modern concept of religiousness.

As we saw earlier, ongoing religious practices—which can be difficult to provide physical proof of—are often disregarded in the cultural World

Heritage system. Faced with the difficulty of presenting material evidence, the Shikoku promotion council chose walking as the central criteria to prove the pilgrimage worthy of World Heritage designation, even though pilgrims on foot are in fact a minority. The promotion council will probably place greater emphasis on this value in future activities. It is likely that the Shikoku Pilgrimage will grow to more closely resemble the Camino de Santiago as efforts are made to expand roads and facilities for pilgrims. Pilgrims from abroad, though still few, are making the pilgrimage on foot, and several books about their experiences have been published. In this respect, the Shikoku Pilgrimage path is an interesting case in the study of the positioning of religious culture in modern society, regardless of whether or not it will be designated as a cultural World Heritage site.

Churches in Nagasaki

Next, let us look at the case of the World Heritage site Hidden Christian Sites in the Nagasaki Region, Japan. These sites have drawn the attention of Japanese religious scholars Kimura Katsuhiko (2007) and Yamanaka Hiroshi (2007), as well as cultural geographer Matsui Keisuke (2013). In 2007, Japan proposed these sites for World Heritage listing, and they were accepted in 2018. Of the Christian sites, what interests us most are religious assets on the Goto Islands off the western coast of Nagasaki Prefecture, of which they are a part. These assets clearly went through a process of "editing" as part of the campaign to obtain World Heritage recognition.

Historically, Christianity first arrived in Japan via missionaries who came to Nagasaki in the sixteenth century. Even today, the prefecture has a large number of Catholic believers. According to 2017 statistics on the sixteen dioceses in Japan, the Nagasaki diocese had 60,362 members, second only to Tokyo, which had 95,484. In a 2017 report entitled "Statistics on the Catholic Church in Japan," the proportion of Catholics to the population was notably high in Nagasaki, about 4.4 percent compared to 0.1 to 0.5 percent in the other dioceses.

It was the Portuguese Jesuit Francis Xavier who started missionary activities in Nagasaki in 1550. Not long afterwards, Catholicism was banned and Christians were persistently oppressed for the next three hundred years, until the Meiji Revolution in 1868 forced Japan to open up to the rest of the world. This oppression is well-documented, for example in the edict to expel Jesuit missionaries issued by Toyotomi Hideyoshi in 1587, the martyrdom of the twenty-six Christians executed in Nagasaki in 1597, and the ban on Christianity issued by the Tokugawa shogunate in 1612.

The struggle of Christians to survive hardship gave birth to a unique religious culture. Catholic believers in Nagasaki went underground to hide their faith. Some pretended to be Buddhists and prayed to statues of the Virgin Mary disguised as Kannon, the Buddhist goddess of mercy. Others developed secret religious communities, whose isolation created a kind of indigenous religion that grew away from Roman Catholicism. In 1873, the Meiji government finally lifted the ban on Christianity, and churches were built at locations where Christians had previously gathered in secret.

As a result, the Nagasaki diocese now has 133 churches, the largest number in Japan (Tokyo has 80 and Yokohama 91), of which 50 are on the Goto Islands, the westernmost part of Kyushu. The islands are not easily accessible even now, and the churches on them are nestled in the depths of mountains or at the tips of capes. In other words, they stand in secluded locations where secret believers prayed during the days of persecution. Today, the churches of Goto still serve as places of worship for local Christians.

Until 2003, when Nagasaki Prefecture and the Catholic Church began their campaign to obtain World Heritage status for this region, these churches were holy spots completely embedded in the local context. During the course of the campaign, however, churches in Goto were given new value as venues for religious tourism.

From the standpoint of sightseeing, the Goto churches, designed by local architect Tetsukawa Yosuke (1879–1976), can be appreciated as a fusion of Japanese and Western architectural styles. Tetsukawa, a Buddhist, learned about Western construction techniques from French missionary Marc Marie de Rotz and went on to design and build more than one third of the churches in the Nagasaki diocese. Because of their histo-

Dogashima Church in Nagasaki.

ry, these churches can claim to have value as tangible objects, similar to other World Heritage sites. They are monuments of cultural exchange between Japan and the West and physical testimony to nineteenth-century globalization, when Japan opened up to the West after a long history of seclusion and rejection of Christianity.

For Catholics, these churches are, more than anything else, a symbol of their strong faith, not just beautiful structures. After the Meiji government lifted Japan's ban on Christianity, churches were built with money raised from donations by missionaries and the forebears of present-day believers. Not only did they donate money, they built the churches with their own hands. For the present-day believers, the churches are a symbol of the hardships their ancestors suffered for more than four hundred years of persecution.

What is interesting about the Nagasaki churches is that a new pilgrimage has been devised to bridge the value they have as material items and the value they have as part of a faith. The Nagasaki pilgrimage was "created" by the Nagasaki Pilgrimage Center, a nonprofit organization, which took the initiative to connect scattered churches into a network of holy spots, similar to the designated temples of the Shikoku Pilgrimage.

This network connects fifty churches dispersed throughout the area. Visitors can obtain a pilgrimage stamp book that looks like the one carried by Camino de Santiago pilgrims. The Center provides tours led by trained pilgrimage guides, and thus the area has been recreated as a sacred world. The Center's official website has an advice page for those visiting a church. The text can be translated as follows:

> A church is "a place of worship." If you know this, you are a pilgrim. You may not be a Catholic believer, but once in a church, you are asked to quietly sit down and close your eyes. After some time, slowly open your eyes . . . You may pray for anything. Do you feel something has been born in your heart? When you go outside the church door, turn back and look at the façade of the building. Does it look different from when you entered? If so, you have experienced your own personal "pilgrimage."

The Center was opened with an archbishop in attendance, but the web posting suggests the Catholic Church has little intention of controlling the Nagasaki pilgrimage according to its doctrine, although it traditionally prescribes guidance for its pilgrimages in detail. For example, in 2007, the Vatican published the following decree granting a plenary indulgence on the 150th anniversary of the apparition of the Blessed Virgin Mary at Lourdes, for believers who carry out the following acts of worship:

> [. . .] during the year running from 8 December 2007 until the end of 8 December 2008, they [believers] devoutly visit the following places, preferably in this order—1) the parish baptismal font used for the Baptism of Bernadette; 2) the house of the Soubirous family called the *cachot*; 3) the Grotto of Massabielle; 4) the chapel of the hospice where Bernadette made her First Communion—and pause to reflect for an appropriate length of time at each of these Jubilee sites, concluding with the Lord's Prayer, some legitimate form of the Profession of Faith, and the Jubilee prayer or some other Marian invocation.

The term *plenary indulgence* means that, simply speaking, Catholics will be pardoned for their sins if they go on a pilgrimage as described in the decree. In other words, it is an official "manual" that teaches the right way to go on a pilgrimage: visit holy places within a specified period in a specified order and pray in a specified manner.

Despite the rigorous traditions of the Catholic church, nonbelievers seem to be accepted rather favorably in Nagasaki. Most visitors to Nagasaki churches are sightseers, who pray in whatever manner they like. In an increasingly secularized and privatized modern society, Catholic churches and sacred places are open to non-Catholics, and individuals are allowed to offer prayers as they wish. The Nagasaki churches have experienced religious change due to their quest for recognition by UNESCO, a nonreligious organization.

The fusion of pilgrimage and tourism does not simply mean that tourism takes advantage of some aspects of religious culture. When touristic and religious contexts merge, tourists begin to perceive religiousness in a new light, and religion transforms in response to the new perception.

Mont-Saint-Michel

Transformation of religion due to the intersecting of sacred and secular worlds is not unique to Japan. Take, for example, the famous French tourist attraction Mont-Saint-Michel, an ancient abbey on a solitary islet off the northern French coast. The structure, perched on a cliff, is widely known as "The Wonder of the Western World" for its beauty. The site was inscribed on the cultural World Heritage List in 1979 as "Mont-Saint-Michel and its Bay," and swarms with millions of tourists from all over the world to this day.

The above description may have given the impression that this is a traditional pilgrimage site; it is not. The building ceased to function as an abbey during the French Revolution and was turned into a prison because of its seclusion. Today, however, when you visit Mont-Saint-Michel, you will see nuns and monks roaming around. They are members of a group formed after the turn of the twentieth century. The group, named the Monastic Fraternities of Jerusalem, was founded in 1975 under the influence of secularization. The intention of the founder Pierre-Marie Delfieux (1934–2013) was to get city-dwellers to rediscover religion. He aimed to give people opportunities to offer prayers or rethink faith in the midst of bustling modern life, for example when visiting churches as

Mont-Saint-Michel.

tourists. The Monastic Fraternities of Jerusalem have their headquarters in Saint-Gervais Church in Le Marais at the center of Paris. Monasteries are usually built away from cities, but many churches and monasteries of this order are located in big cities and tourist destinations. In addition to Mont-Saint-Michel, the group has communities in Strasbourg and Vézelay, both World Heritage sites in France, as well as in Rome, Florence, Brussels and Montreal.

The Monastic Fraternities of Jerusalem have been associated with Mont-Saint-Michel since 2001, when they moved to the abbey to restore it as a place of worship at the request of the local bishop. The buildings and assets, however, belong to France and are managed by the French government. In other words, the group members live in the world-famous tourist destination, exposed to the eyes of tourists from countries around the world. This is quite different from the image of a traditional monastery. The presence of the Fraternities at Mont-Saint-Michel may well be regarded as an example of change caused by the fusion of religion and tourism.

Repositioning religious culture in society

In this chapter, we have considered the fusion of religion and tourism in modern society from the standpoint of the World Heritage system. Many cases have shown that religion is transforming under the influence of secular criteria established by UNESCO, a nonreligious organization. Local faith, individual belief, or religious culture can be processed to prove universal value, and in this process, some aspects of tradition are removed, or new traditions created.

Inscription on the World Heritage List means that local sites and traditions are put under the scrutiny of UNESCO's global criteria. In this process, sites whose value is obvious to locals are put on the table and compared with others. In many cases, World Heritage sites contain multiple assets, but often some are removed from the constituent elements of a designated site during UNESCO's examination because the proposing countries or municipal governments have failed to sufficiently prove their value. In this sense, the process of selection and editing described in this chapter exerts a sort of brute force on religious culture.

This, however, does not mean that religious culture is processed and sold simply as merchandise for tourists. Through the process of fusion between religion and tourism, both redefine themselves and begin to coexist with a new sense of distance from each other. In a secularized society, religion no longer comes to the fore as dominant culture or value. For many people, religion is not a major aspect of their existence.

In a secular world, the cultural World Heritage system provides important channels for the repositioning of religion in society. Through secular criteria and evaluation, religion regains value as a culture that is worthy of everyone's appreciation.

Making a Sacred Spot: How Authenticity Is Born of a Sham

Chapter 4

This chapter centers on the case of the village of Shingo in Aomori Prefecture, in northern Japan. In the 1930s, the villagers happened to hear a legend that Jesus Christ had come to Japan. This was followed by the "discovery" of Christ's tomb in the village. The story is so absurd that Shingo and its Christ legend are treated almost as a joke and widely referred to as a second-rate tourist attraction.

Both history and religion make it hard to accept the authenticity of the tomb. Stories told by the locals, however, reveal some special sentiments toward this historical sham. This suggests that even something so obviously counterfeit can become a holy place because of the subjective interpretation of the people associated with it.

The case of Shingo shows the importance of perception and experience when it comes to judging the authenticity of a holy place. It also offers an important clue to understanding pilgrimage in an increasingly privatized modern society.

Shingo and the legend of Christ

The village of Shingo (called Herai until 1955), a hamlet with a single traffic signal, is near the southern border of Aomori Prefecture (fig. 3). Shingo's population peaked at about 5,000 in the 1970s after which it began to decline. By April 2018 it held only 2,547 people in 935 households. It was here that the legend of Christ grew out of a notorious hoax.

This hoax revolves around the Takeuchi Documents, which are said to be ancient manuscripts passed down through the family of Takeuchi Kiyomaro (1875–1965), the founder of a religious movement called

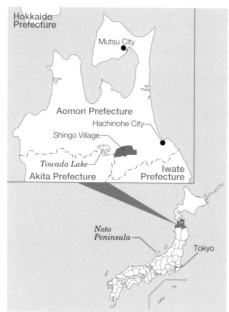

Figure 3:
Shingo Village, Aomori
Prefecture.

Amatsukyo. The manuscripts form the holy book of the religion, and Takeuchi claimed that the historical events they describe are true. Most of what is written in the Takeuchi Documents, first brought to light in 1910, is thought to be Takeuchi's work. While it covers a wide range of topics, the book advocates a worldview that "Japan is the fundamental source of everything that exists on the earth" (Kume 2012).

For example, the documents claim that major cities, such as New York and Boston, were built by a family of brothers from Japan who were dispersed around the globe a few thousand years ago. The papers also assert that religious figures and philosophers, such as Buddha, Confucius, Mencius, and Moses, were all trained in Japan in their youth.

Such a view of the world was nurtured in the 1930s, in the years leading to World War II. In ancient times, Japan felt inferior to Chinese civilization and then, after the Meiji Restoration in 1868, was forced to play second fiddle to the West. Reversing Japan's position must have been on Takeuchi's mind when he insisted that all Western civilizations had their roots in ancient Japan, and that Japan was the world's leader and source of all cultures. To further promote this historical view, Takeuchi made up the legend that Christ lived in the village of Shingo. The discovery of Christ's tomb there was considered physical evidence.

In October 1934, Sasaki Denjiro, headman of then Herai Village, invited Toya Banzan, a well-known artist and man of culture, to serve as the face of a village development scheme planned around a government project to designate the Towada Lake area as a national park. Banzan was originally from Aomori and often made the lake the subject of his paintings. Toya accepted Sasaki's invitation, but he had his own agenda. An avid reader of the Takeuchi Documents, Toya spent his time in Herai trying to prove that an ancient holy town had once existed there. Toya then claimed that a local rock, known as Oishi-gami (the big-rock god), was actually a pyramid.

About six months prior to Toya's visit to Herai, another "pyramid" had been discovered in Hiroshima. Sakai Katsutoki, a Christian inspired by the Takeuchi Documents, had made the find, which got into the newspapers and became a topic of conversation. According to the Takeuchi Documents, there were seven pyramids in Japan, all predating those in Egypt. Sakai and Toya each believed they had found one of the seven.

In August 1935, Toya invited Takeuchi and some others to Herai to closely examine his discovery. On this, his second trip, Toya took meticulous notes and used them to write a book that he published the following year. From this book, we learn that members of the group were treated as honored guests and stayed at the homes of local established families, politicians, and military personnel. On the morning of August 7 the group headed for Toya's Oishi-gami pyramid upon the request of Takeuchi. The tomb of Christ was discovered on the way, when they climbed a twelve-meter hill and found two burial mounds in a row. Takeuchi offered a silent prayer to the mounds and then declared, "This is the place!" He then headed for Oishi-gami where he silently prayed again, and announced that this was indeed "the place." That night, thirty people, including villagers, came to a gathering held at an inn. Takeuchi and his peers questioned the locals about village folktales and local place names. From the next day on, Herai was considered a "holy" town.

There were no Christians in Herai in 1935 and none have lived there

The tomb of Christ in Shingo Village.

since. Nor was there even a folktale related to the underground Christians who had existed elsewhere in the country since the sixteenth century. The villagers heard the legend out of the blue from these two outsiders: some called it a *yosetsu*, "a legend that sprang up" like water. These days, few villagers survive who had direct contact with either Toya or Takeuchi. Yet people have passed the stories of their visits down through the generations, and still talk about them now. They still use the words "big black cars" (a rare sight in those days), leading to speculation that Takeuchi was accompanied by notable persons in official vehicles, such as scholars, politicians, and military personnel who sympathized with the view of history expressed in the Takeuchi Documents. In those days, the village was far more remote and isolated than it is today. It must have been a shock for the locals to have these mysterious strangers barging into their life and suddenly declaring their hometown to be the resting place of a world religious leader.

The New Testament gives no account of the period from the birth of Jesus Christ to the time he started religious activities in his thirties. The Takeuchi Documents claim that when Jesus Christ was twenty-one years old, he came to Japan, landing on the Noto Peninsula, which juts out into the Sea of Japan. He then learned Japanese—the language of "Heaven"—and pursued theological training. He went back to Israel at age thirty-three and propagated the teachings he had learned in Japan. His preaching made Jewish elders so angry that they arrested Jesus and condemned him to death on the cross. Jesus' younger brother, whose name was Isukiri, took his place on the cross, and Jesus fled with his disciples across Siberia to the East. He finally returned to Japan, landing at the port of Hachinohe in Aomori. He settled in the Sawaguchi neighborhood of Herai, where Takeuchi found his tomb. In Herai, Jesus changed his name to Torai Taro Daitenku, married a twenty-year-old Japanese woman called Miyuko, fathered three daughters, and lived to the ripe old age of 106. While in Japan, Jesus traveled extensively. His unfamiliar facial features gave rise to legends of *tengu*, long-nosed goblins, in this region of Japan.

Most of the Takeuchi Documents were lost in a crackdown on the Amatsukyo religion in 1935. Takeuchi's papers discussed history predating Emperor Jinmu, the legendary first emperor of Japan—something that would have been considered treasonous in prewar imperial Japan— and Takeuchi also claimed to possess papers written by ancient emperors Chokei and Godaigo. Takeuchi was indicted for lèse-majesté, but at the end of World War II, he received a not-guilty verdict. Unfortunately, the courthouse where his documents were stored was burned down in an air raid. After the war was over, no one outside the village paid any attention to the supposed tomb of Christ for some time.

The legend of Christ after World War II

A village woman in her seventies remembers a postwar childhood outing to the tomb of Christ. After walking through a thicket to reach it, she saw two burial mounds, which in those days were not marked with crosses as they are now. She also recalls village officials going around houses looking for relics that might have been related to the legend and thus useful for promoting the village.

Years passed, and the tomb came into the spotlight again during the "occult boom" of the 1970s. In 1973, an article titled "Jesus Christ Died in Japan" appeared in the *Mainichi Graphic Weekly* (December 23 issue). It reported the legend of Christ as given in the Takeuchi Documents and talked about old village customs assumed to be connected to the

Christian practices that Jesus brought. For instance, to ward off bad luck, mothers would draw a cross in charcoal on the foreheads of their babies the first time they were taken outside. The article also contained large photos of unusual farm clothing called *harade* and the village Bon Festival dance featuring *nanyadoyara* folk songs, which were allegedly derived from Hebrew.

The tone of this article is what made it noteworthy. It treated the preposterous legend as a joke and declared that there were no Christians in the village. Local people who were interviewed all stated that no one in the village believed in the legend of Christ.

Around the year 2000, the construction of Home of Christ Park began in the village. Two burial mounds sit on top of the park's highest hill. One is Toraizuka, which is said to be the tomb of Jesus Christ. The other is Judaibo, which contains the hair and other relics of Jesus' younger brother Isukiri, who took Jesus's place on the cross. Isukiri, of course, is not mentioned in the New Testament. In the park is a small museum operated by a village-funded corporation. In addition to local traditions and customs, the museum displays the last will and testament of Christ and other exhibits related to the legend that sprang up from the Takeuchi Documents. Opposite the two burial mounds is the grave of the Sawaguchi family, who donated their land for the park. Local legend has it that the Sawaguchis were descended from Christ. The museum displays their portraits, complete with chiseled non-Asian features, as proof of their sacred lineage.

The tomb of Christ draws its greatest number of visitors during the Christ Festival on the first Sunday of June each year. This festival started in 1964 on the initiative of the chief priest of Herai Mitaki Shrine. It was initially run by the local chamber of commerce, and is now sponsored by Shingo's tourist association. The village headman plays the role of festival chief accompanied by the chairman of the local tourist bureau and the head of the Sawaguchi family, who—as a supposed descendant—takes care of the tomb.

True Christianity teaches that Jesus Christ went to heaven after his resurrection, so there is no practice of comforting his mortal spirit, as in the Shinto religion. Shingo's Christ Festival, however, is conducted in

The museum in Home of Christ Park.

Shinto style, aimed at consoling the soul of Jesus. Although there have been minor variations over the years, the festival takes the form of a memorial service: it opens with a Shinto prayer recited by the chief priest (Plate 16), followed by speeches by guests such as members of the National Diet and the municipal assembly. Next, sacred sprigs of *sakaki*, a variety of camellia, are offered on the altar, in keeping with Shinto funeral practices (Plate 15). Then there is a performance of the traditional Tanaka *shishimai* lion dance and an award ceremony for *tanka* poems composed on the theme of Christ's tomb. The climax of the eighty-minute ceremony is the nanyadoyara dancing around the tomb by village women (Plate 14).

Nanyadoyara are traditional Bon festival songs sung in the southern part of Aomori and the northern parts of Iwate and Akita prefectures. The voice modulation and instruments vary by region, but the cryptic lyrics "nanyadoyara, nanyadonasareno, nanyadoyara" have been handed down from ancient times.

The words have been interpreted in many ways. For example, Yanagita Kunio (1875–1962), the father of Japanese native folkloristics, thought they were "songs of love" (Yanagita 1926). In the Christ Festival, the village announces that the songs are derived from Hebrew. This is based on a theory from doctor of Divinity Kawamorita Eiji (1891–1960) who claims that in Hebrew the words mean praise to Jehovah, god of the Israelites (Kawamorita 1956).

In Shingo, nanyadoyara was once on the brink of extinction, as the dwindling village population was unable to produce dancers. However, the Christ Festival provides a good opportunity for public performance, so the society Folkways of Shingo was founded to preserve this traditional art (Yamada 2011). At the fiftieth Christ Festival in 2013, following the regular spirit-consoling service, a nanyadoyara gala was held by nine conservation societies from outside the village. In Shingo visitors can also buy nanyadoyara CDs with commentaries and nanyadoyara remixes by different artists in bossa nova and techno styles.

The tomb of Christ as a tourist attraction

In Shingo, whose population is about two thousand five hundred, the tomb of Christ is the only tourist attraction and the Christ Festival is the only event that includes the entire village in its scope. It draws up to a thousand people, with nonresidents outnumbering the locals.

The annual number of visitors to the village tops ten thousand (a third from outside Japan), most of whom head for the tomb of Christ, according to the Shingo revitalization corporation. The village's official tourist leaflet carries photos of the tomb, Christ's last will and testament, and nanyadoyara dancers around the burial mounds, under the headings "History of the Home of Christ" and "Invitation to the Mysterious Hamlet." Aomori Prefecture is also promoting itself as a place for healing, with the catchphrase *michi-no-kuni* (beautiful land of the unknown). Their tourist brochure recommends twenty-one mysterious places, including Christ's tomb in Shingo, as well as thirty-seven power spots in Aomori. Shingo has distinguished itself from neighboring towns as a place worth visiting, thanks to the tomb of Christ.

As we have seen, the tomb of Christ and its festival grew out of a false history, and their development as tourist resources was spurred by the occult boom and Shingo's revitalization activities. To promote tourism, the village also features other dubious legends, such as the Oishi-gami pyramid discovered by Toya and Takeuchi.

The so-called pyramid is a rocky hillock on a mountain about a

Oishi-gami pyramid.

ten-minute drive westward from the tomb of Christ. The placard set up by the village says that "pyramid expert" Sakai Katsutoki (who discovered the pyramid in Hiroshima), endorsed it as a place where one can imagine the existence of a prehistoric holy town. Some nearby boulders are given names, such as Compass Rock, which has cracks made precisely in the four cardinal directions, and Constellation Rock, which points towards the North Star.

Further to the west is Mount Towari, which according to Takeuchi, was Japan's oldest pyramid and an ancient place of sun worship. The starting point of a trail up this mountain is a forested area called Mayoga-tai, which was once claimed to be the Garden of Eden by Yamane Kiku, an activist for women's suffrage in the Taisho era (1912–1926). Yamane was influenced by Takeuchi and spread the legends of Shingo village in her own books (Yamane 1937).

Religious culture born out of a sham

Shingo's Christ legend has been embraced by people with strong imaginations and a taste for the supernatural. Since the rise of the occult boom in the 1970s, the legend has been featured in numerous magazines, romantic stories, and comics, including novels by Saito Sakae and Takahashi Katsuhiko, as well as travel literature by Kosaka Shunji.

Zooming forward to the present day, with the Internet widespread, there are now a variety of websites that introduce Christ's tomb as a second-rate tourist attraction and its festival as a peculiarity. These websites treat the tomb as a place with no historical or religious authenticity. Yet there are some visitors who seem to find a sort of authenticity here. Some dance around the tomb to receive energy, while others meditate at the model pyramid in front of the village museum. To such people, the tomb seems to be a "power spot" where they feel some sort of spiritual force.

For the past few years, the tomb's staircase has been decorated with flowers on the Christ Festival day. The flowers are sent every year by a woman from out of the prefecture. She had suffered a serious disease and visited holy places around the world to pray for her recovery—all in vain. The final site she went to was the tomb of Christ in Shingo, after which she was healed. Since then, this woman has donated flowers to express her gratitude, and the story of her restored health is announced every year during the festival. This demonstrates that there are people who find something religious or mysterious about the tomb, regardless of whether they believe in the legend of Christ coming to Japan.

This said, the most prominent characteristic of the tomb is that neither villagers nor visitors strongly assert its historical or religious authenticity. Many villagers are aware of how the legend originated and how it

People receiving energy from the tomb.

has been used as a tourist resource in the postwar era. Despite the fact that the Christ Festival is held to comfort the soul of Christ, many invited speakers end their speeches with congratulatory words, such as "Happy Christ Festival Day!" The finale is a grand toast of apple juice, made from renowned Aomori apples. The unreal atmosphere is probably what makes participants so ready to enjoy this festivity born of a bizarre legend.

For the villagers, however, the tomb and the festival are not simply commercial assets for promoting tourism. The Christ Festival has affected village life on both cultural and emotional levels.

First, let's look at the influence the Christ Festival has had on the village's folk art. The festival attracts many people who expect to witness a bizarre occult ritual performed by believers. More than a few visitors therefore are disappointed when they experience the festival, which is more like a traditional Japanese festival and not strange at all in its individual elements, except that the opening Shinto prayer is offered for Jesus Christ.

Most of the festival is taken up with Tanaka shishimai and nanyadoyara dances. As mentioned earlier, the numbers of nanyadoyara dancers had been decreasing until the founding of the festival prompted the formation of a preservation society. The Tanaka shishimai lion dance, previously performed at the Herai Mitaki Shrine festival, is now performed during the Christ Festival. Thus, the fake event contributed to reviving and spreading folk dances previously unknown outside the village. We can say the Christ Festival has transformed folk art into tourist culture.

In a magazine interview, the village headman said, "When a local women's group created a nanyadoyara dance for the Christ Festival, the village bought drums to support them." He used the word "created" for nanyadoyara, the traditional village music that was once at the risk of dying out. His word is not a misunderstanding of fact, but rather reflects changes in people's perceptions. We can assume that, thanks to the Christ Festival, this folk art has grown in such a way as to make the locals see it as an original creation.

Emotional attachment to Christ's burial site is found in the words of festival staff, village officials, and volunteers from regional development groups. When talking about this spot, they make it clear that some significant person, if not Christ himself, must be buried there. In fact, the burial mound had always been important to the villagers since before its "discovery" by Takeuchi.

The Herai Mitaki Shrine priest, who conducts the Shinto ritual at the Christ Festival, affirms the importance of consoling the spirit of the deceased, whomever that may be. Should Jesus Christ actually be resting in the tomb, there would be no problem, the priest says, because Shinto is a religion that endorses all the gods of heaven and earth.

Explaining why the Christ Festival is conducted in the Shinto style, one village official and festival staff member said, "Shinto gods are superior to Buddha." In this village, he explains, Shinto priests are thought to be descendants of *yamabushi* mountain ascetics and are called *betto*, a term used for local residents with the highest social status. Betto are therefore best suited to preside over the festival. The official said he did not think that the body of Christ was in the tomb, but he believed the person buried there was his ancestor in a broad sense of the word, so the traditional memorial service ought to be continued.

These narratives show that the tomb of Christ is not merely an attraction to lure in sightseers. Rather than argue over the historical authenticity of the tomb or the legend, villagers feel affection for this place handed down through generations. Such a feeling is revealed in their angry response to an article that appeared in a major newspaper in 2012. The article discusses the geographical features of the area around the tomb of Christ and identifies it as the site of a castle built by a member of the indigenous ethnic group in northern Japan known as the Emishi. According to the article, the person buried in the tomb was a *matsurowa-nu-mono*, or rebel, who disobeyed the central sovereign and fought for the independence of the region. The article concludes that the prayers given in the Christ Festival has some connection to the Emishi because Jesus Christ was also a matsurowanu-mono whom Jews considered to be a heretic. After briefly touching on the Christ legend, the article ends with the sentence, "I wonder what the 'person conveniently renamed Christ' is thinking in his tomb" (Asahi Shimbun 2012).

People involved with the festival criticized this article as both one-sided and high-handed. Interestingly, most locals are aware of how the Christ legend sprang up and understand that the article's Emishi theory is a more acceptable historical viewpoint. Yet, they strongly objected to the article. One villager gave the following comment:

> I grew up hearing people tell me the place is the tomb of Christ. But all of a sudden this article claims it was "a castle built by the Emishi." It doesn't ring true. For us, the place is Christ's tomb, nothing else. I know we are descended from the Emishi, but it doesn't make any difference. It's nothing other than the tomb of Christ. That's what it says on maps.
>
> Earthenware was in fact dug up on a hill above the village Museum. The hill was called *tate*, which means "castle," so a castle might have stood there once. But the excavation site is quite a distance from the burial site. Not only that, but the mounds of the tombs are below the hill. That's strange, and I'll tell you why. When I visited another of our village graveyards this year, I saw two burial mounds just like that of Christ, at the highest spot in their graveyard. All the other gravestones were placed below them. This follows the practice of our ancestors, who dug their graves below the Christ mounds out of respect.
>
> If someone built a castle above the Christ tomb, that person must have been an outsider, not a native of this land. For generations, we have been told to treasure the tomb because it's the resting place of an important person. No natives would think of building a house above it. Some may argue the castle owner built a family grave there, but it's unlikely because families don't build graves below their houses.
>
> The article is written with no regard for the respect we feel for our ancestors.
>
> (Based on an interview by the author with a villager in his 40s)

As you can see here, villagers do not care which is historically correct—the Christ legend or the Emishi theory. What matters most appears to be that the legend has been handed down from generation to generation. The Emishi theory caused resentment not because of its historical viewpoint but because of the absence of a relevant legend.

An Aomori prefectural official engaged in village tourism regards the

Christ Festival as a venue for folk entertainment such as the nanyadoyara and Tanaka shishimai dances. He sees the fifty-year-old festival as a tradition. Local people feel connected to their forefathers through the passing down of the Christ legend and the holding of the festival, so the content of the festival itself does not mean much.

Academically, the tomb of Christ is judged to be a fake. Regardless of this, however, it connects villagers to their ancestors. It is a holy place in a sense that it gives local people a regional identity. Looking closely at the emphasis local interviewees placed on blood relations and regional ties, we can say that these two elements also make the tomb authentic.

Villagers' perceptions of the tomb of Christ are interesting when considering how a sense of belonging to the land or community is created. Sociologist Osawa Masachi claims that community is not born of a shared belief: "A collection of individuals is regarded as a community when they all presume that *others* share a common belief" (Osawa 2009).

The majority of Shingo residents deny the historical authenticity of the legend of Christ and any relationship between village customs and Jewish culture. They stress, however, that the tomb of Christ has long been cherished as a special spot. In other words, villagers think it important to "believe in people who once believed in the authenticity of the tomb." Their stance is to respect the efforts of the people who tended the tomb in the past.

This attitude is sustained by a sense of belonging and of having ties to the community, including its ancestry. The tomb of Christ has a history that is so phony that villagers themselves are unable to believe in it. The sham is obvious particularly to those who are closest and know the most about it, such as festival officials and members of tourism promotion groups. This is exactly why they emphasize their unity based on regional and blood ties inherited from their forebears.

Subjective authenticity

Chapter 1 discussed the authenticity of tourist spots and holy places from an academic viewpoint—with a focus on physical integrity. This was an objective approach. The case of the Christ legend of Shingo, on the other hand, shows the necessity of considering subjective elements, such as the awareness and emotions of people associated with a particular place. Let's examine the legend of Christ—which is based on a hoax—from the conventional approach of discussing whether something is genuine or fake.

Conventional discussions on pilgrimages and tourism see the two as incompatible. As early as 1961, the superficial nature of sightseeing was criticized by historian Daniel J. Boorstin in his book *The Image: A Guide to Pseudo-events in America*. This book discusses the degradation of American society at a time when the media was beginning to gain power and conceal facts using illusions in various social spheres. Boorstin gives tourism as a typical example of something that is replete with illusion. He says tourist destinations are filled with artificial pseudo-ideal images and specious simplifications. Boorstin claims that what we see is not natural but deliberately designed. Tourists are unable to see that pseudo-events are false; they would rather find pleasure in consuming them.

Boorstin's argument is significant in that it drew attention to the way media had begun to manipulate images. His argument, however, resembles the most superficial understanding of the legend of Christ. That is, the false legend and the tomb were intentionally created to stimulate tourism, and have been consumed by those swept along by the trend for visiting the sites of supernatural events and second-rate tourist attractions. Such a viewpoint prevents us from understanding the authenticity that is derived from people's affection for ancestral sites and folklore. For Boorstin, only academic criteria are used to distinguish real from fake (Boorstin 1961).

Next, let's look at the theory of tourism sociologist Dean MacCannell, who argues that tourists attempt to go "backstage" in search of authenticity. MacCannell classifies tourism into six stages, presented here in somewhat simplified form. First is the main stage designed for tourism. Second is the stage created to appear to be the backstage but which only has a "backstage atmosphere." Third is the front-stage simulation that is totally created to appear to be a backstage. Fourth is the backstage that is partly open to outsiders. Fifth is the backstage that may be cleaned up or slightly altered because tourists are permitted an occasional glimpse. Sixth is an actual backstage, the kind of place that tourists are looking for.

While not denying the deliberately created and staged authenticity of tourist spots, MacCannell defines tourists as individuals who are not satisfied with the main stage but attempt to go behind it in search of things as they really are. In short, tourists are active beings who want to participate in the lives of their hosts (MacCannell 1976).

Anthropologist Nelson Graburn argues that daily life is in fact a fabrication and one can expect to have more intense experiences only at travel destinations. According to Graburn, sightseeing provides an opportunity for an individual to escape a superficial secular space, namely, monotonous modern life. In this sense, tourism is a sacred journey, where tourists can experience authenticity even in specially created tourist spots (Graburn 1977).

Let's consider the Christ Festival based upon these arguments. Presided over by a priest at an altar, this "festival" is in effect an event sponsored by the village tourist bureau. The traditional nanyadoyara dance was revived for the sake of the festival. Boorstin would call it a deliberately staged pseudo-event. However, the locals perceive the festival as a bona fide tradition. Meanwhile, visitors are not deceived by the sham either. They often ask festival staff and Shinto priests about the origin of the festival and how they should pray at the tomb. They learn that while the person buried is unknown, the tomb is considered a cherished ancestral site. Thus active interchange between the local people and the visitors is one of the major characteristics of the Christ Festival.

Japan has "real" festivals throughout the country, such as the Nebuta Matsuri in Aomori, the Gion Matsuri in Kyoto, and the Kishiwada Danjiri Matsuri in Osaka. The traditional authenticity of these events is widely accepted. They are conducted on a much greater scale, though, and seem to offer fewer opportunities for visitors—who come from around the country to see them—to mingle with locals. There is no reason for visitors to doubt the authenticity of the festivals, so they accept the images created by television programs and travel guides. With the eyes of outsiders, they appreciate the festival as it is staged. Indeed, all three of these festivals have bleachers set up for visitors who pay to sit there. This means there is no place for tourists to mix with the locals. The bleachers keep visitors focused on the main stage. The Christ Festival, on the other hand, permits tourists a glimpse of the backstage precisely because it is founded on a sham.

Social anthropologist Erik Cohen has identified five modes of tourist experience—recreational, diversionary, experiential, experimental, and existential—that can help us consider the question of interchange between locals and visitors. Cohen argues that sightseeing experiences can have a depth and intensity that can be called religious, and the key point is interpersonal exchange. In recreational mode, tourists travel for pleasure. They set no serious goals and enjoy traveling as entertainment. Similarly, in diversionary mode, people travel in order to relieve boredom.

The other three modes are different. In experiential mode, tourists who have found no meaning in life meet somebody during their journey and learn from their way of life, but only as observers. In experimental mode, travelers gain a more profound experience, absorbing somebody's way of life as a principle that guides their own lives. Finally, the deepest experience is attained in existential mode, where even more drastic changes occur. Because of a journey, a traveler chooses a way of life completely different from the one they led in their own society or culture. This kind of trip alters a person's existence, so that they end up living in a foreign land. Cohen discusses journeys in existential mode as something close to a conversion through religious awakening (Cohen 1998).

The tomb of Christ shows how ambiguous the boundary between the real and the fake can be. Subjective authenticity perceived by both locals and visitors is gaining importance in the study of modern pilgrimages. This is because societies no longer share a single value or worldview due to the progress of secularization and privatization.

In a secularized society, not all people recognize even ancient historical sites as holy ground. In the Roman Catholic Church, the Cathedral of Santiago de Compostela is regarded as the third-most sacred spot, following Jerusalem and Rome. Yet these days, when churches are losing influence, the historical background and authority of the cathedral are not the only factors that make it a pilgrimage site. Today, many people walking toward this holy place are pilgrims who do not have religious faith.

To put it the other way around, in modern times, an ordinary place with no tradition sometimes turns out to be a sacred spot. New meaning may be given to a holy place worshipped by only a limited group of people or a place considered not sacred at all in the first place. The sentiments and subjective engagement of the people involved are what are important, as well as the mingling of tourists with locals. The tomb of Christ can be interpreted as a typical example of such a holy place.

Chapter 5

My Own Private Sacred Site: Power Spots and Diversity of Prayer

This chapter discusses "power spots" in Japan, which have been enjoying a boom since the turn of the twenty-first century. We will see how a holy place is born in modern society, sometimes under the influence of mass media. The power-spot boom is a good example of how religion has become privatized. We see a place transform into a sacred spot as stories and rituals are created to lure people into becoming active pilgrims.

Japanese sacred sites and their backgrounds

The term *power-spot boom* is used here to describe a sudden proliferation of sacred spots. Before studying this boom in Japan, we must understand two major characteristics of the country's religious culture—the prevalence of animism and the absence of religious supervisory institutions—both of which make it easier to establish holy places in Japan than in Christian societies, and are thus also a factor in the recent boom in the number of "sacred sites."

First, let's look at the religious belief called animism. In short, it is a view of the world in which all things possess souls. The Japanese attitude toward religion is characterized by the belief that all creatures—human, animal, plant, and even inorganic objects—have souls. In particular, Japanese people see gods and spirits in nature. Rocks, caves, and trees are perceived as having wills and spirits, as are natural forces such as rain, wind, and lightning. Typical examples are Mount Fuji and other high mountains; giant waterfalls, such as the one in Kumano Nachi Grand Shrine; and the massive boulders in Sefa-utaki. Christian culture, on the other hand, tends to have a negative attitude toward animism, saying that

Tamaya Shrine was built as part of a cave on Mount Hidehikosan.

there is only one God, and it was this deity who designed and created the world.

Animism caught the attention of Sir Edward Tylor (1832–1917), the British scholar called the father of anthropology. Tylor developed an evolutionary framework for religion, in which monotheism was the apex. Animism was regarded as the simplest form of religion, as it perceived souls in all living things.

If we look at pilgrimages in the Christian world, however, we actually can find animistic imagination behind these religious practices. Chapter 1 of this book, for example, discusses relics venerated by Christians. Such veneration is obviously based on beliefs that special power resides in the objects themselves. Many of the appearances made by the Virgin Mary are in locations that inspire animistic worship, such as the mountain top of Notre-Dame de La Salette and the grotto in Lourdes. Alphonse Dupront, an eminent French authority on pilgrimage studies, has pointed out that as late as the nineteenth century, the French had a great reverence for mountains and a fear of venturing into them. The fact that

Mary of Lourdes made her appearance in the mountains of the Pyrenees enhanced the reverent feelings of pilgrims.

The second characteristic of religion in Japan is the absence of religious institutions that control influences exerted by animistic beliefs. As discussed earlier, miracles such as Marian apparitions are a double-edged sword for the Roman Catholic Church. This is because the church is presided over by the Pope, who embodies the power of the one true God on earth. In other words, authority is concentrated in a single person. Miracles such as apparitions attract people, but can threaten the authority of religious leaders. In some cases the Virgin Mary criticizes the Pope, but of course, such apparitions are not authenticated. This is why any miracle, whether it be a holy apparition or the deeds of a saint, is thoroughly scrutinized by the church.

Animism has recently been reviewed in positive contexts, giving birth to a sort of religious nationalism in Japan. Tylor and other religious researchers in the West used the concept of animism to discuss non-Christian "inferior religions" in non-Western countries. Meanwhile, Japanese anthropologist Iwata Keiji and philosopher Umehara Takeshi have praised animism as a religious idea unique to Japan. They say that Shintoism and Buddhism based on animism have a universality that transcends mere religious systems and organizations because they aim at living in harmony with nature. For example, the Sacred Island of Okinoshima and Associated Sites in the Munakata Region, in its application for World Heritage status was recommended because of its universal value as a spot sacred to animism. Some argue that animism is still alive and well in contemporary Japanese culture. American anthropologist Anne Allison has analyzed the Japanese imagination through anime and video games—involving Astro Boy, Godzilla, and Pokemon, to name just a few—and uses the term "techno animism" to discuss how people find "life" in machines such as robots and police cars (Allison 2006).

Japan has no central institutions that control Shinto gods, Buddhist deities, or faith in miracles. Shinto has no founder, although Amaterasu-omikami, the sun goddess ancestor of the imperial family, is regarded as its chief deity. In effect, people worship innumerable gods who protect local communities or particular occupations. Not only that, but Shinto also has elements of ancestral rites. Some experts have tried to establish Shinto doctrines, but their efforts have not made headway with the general public. In Japan, faith has been passed down through practices such as festivals and annual celebrations, and there is no structured belief system like that of Christianity. Animistic views find holiness in everything and there are no institutions that centrally control sacred objects. In short, people are not as inhibited about making up so-called holy items in Japan as in the Christian culture, meaning sacred sites can sprout up rather easily.

"Celebrity gods" in the age of information

The designation of sacred spots dates back as far as the Edo period (1603–1868), when a local god would suddenly became popular. Let's examine these phenomena as a clue to understanding power-spot booms in modern times. Anthropologist Miyata Noboru studied *hayarigami*, or "celebrity gods," who came into popular favor one after the other during the Edo era and later (Miyata 1993). These fads were spurred by the imaginations of people who lived in an increasingly urbanized society.

Celebrity gods sometimes gained immense popularity overnight even though they did not belong to famous shrines or temples. More often than not, people were whipped into a religious frenzy over a *yashiki-gami* (an "estate god," one worshipped in a private home) or a tiny village shrine that had been revered only by a small group of residents. A typical example, says Miyata, is Taro Inari, a shrine in Taito-ku, Tokyo, a *yashiki-gami* of the Tachibana family, a feudal clan. Although there is no sign of it left today, Taro Inari enjoyed incredible popularity several times during the Edo period and as recently as the early twentieth century. At the crest of each boom, Taro Inari received countless banners and lanterns from donors. Miyata illustrates the process of the emergence of a celebrity god as follows: a revelation is communicated through somebody's dream, and then a deity comes flying in, or a figurine of a god or Buddha is discovered on the beach or dug up from the ground. Next, people start talking about some miraculous power or good fortune, or a person possessed delivers divine messages. This is how a celebrity god is begotten. This scheme is helpful when considering the power-spot phenomenon these days.

In addition to celebrity gods, Miyata also refers to the tales of human-faced dogs, fish, and trees that were popular in the 1980s and 90s. There was an urban legend in the Tokyo region of talking dogs with human faces. Carp in the pond of Zenpoji Temple in Tsuruoka, Yamagata Prefecture were also believed to have human faces, attracting crowds of people to the pond, where sweet buns stamped with the fish face were sold as souvenirs. As for the tree version, a zelkova tree in a park in Yachiyo, Chiba Prefecture has a gash in the trunk that looks like a human face. The tree is called Yurino-ki-kannon (tree goddess) by local residents. A rumor started to circulate that your prayers could be answered if you touched the trunk. As a result of this rumor, the tree was bound with a *shimenawa* straw rope, indicating a sacred Shinto place, and an offertory chest was set up nearby. Following the emergence of these attractions, similar human-faced fish and trees were discovered in many places across Japan and came briefly into the spotlight. Miyata says that the "human-face" boom was created by rumors bred in the age of information.

Mass media and information dissemination via the Internet play a significant role in power-spot booms in the twenty-first century. Religious sociologists Tsukada Hotaka and Omi Toshihiro point out that a power-spot boom begins with the extensive proliferation of a large amount of information about a holy place. In other words, it is an information event (Tsukada and Omi 2011). In this respect, Miyata's scheme can be simplified as follows:

Holy object or place × enhancement and dissemination of information → celebrity god

With this scheme in mind, we can say the nature of a so-called holy object or place has remained unchanged since the end of the Edo period in 1868. As we will see later in this chapter, most of today's power spots are also shrines, temples, and sacred sites where gods have long been worshipped. The difference lies in the increasing amount of information and diversified ways it is disseminated. With power-spot phenomena, a holy place is hardly ever created from scratch by a god or a deity who performs a miracle.

Accordingly, when we think of a power spot, its location is not as important as the way in which its story has been "edited" and "staged." Note that a power spot is not edited or staged to withstand academic scrutiny based on objective criteria. Some shrines and temples intentionally orchestrate the impressions they make, while others ignore or object to any such maneuvering. In some cases, visitors create new images and practices.

Next, we will discuss power-spot phenomena in the twenty-first century more concretely. Since the location of power spots do not mean much, it is meaningless to classify them by region. The important thing is how the image of a place is edited or presented in a new light. I will discuss three types of power spots—renamed, reinforced, and discovered. The focus is on *who* is using the label "power spot."

Renamed power spots

This term refers to traditional holy places that have been renamed as power spots. Many of the newly spotlighted power spots are in effect long-recognized sacred places, including well-known shrines, head temples of Buddhist sects, and other holy grounds in Japan. It would take all day to name them, but they include Atsuta Shrine, Iwashimizu Hachimangu Shrine, Kasuga Grand Shrine, Kashima Shrine, Togakushi Shrine, Mount Koya, and Mount Hiei. In addition, the Ise Shrines and Izumo Grand Shrine are also referred to as power spots these days.

The Ise Shrines, the most sacred Shinto shrines in Japan, which have long been a tourist destination, are a good example. The shrine complex is rebuilt every twenty years, and it draws large crowds the year its main shrine is completed. Recently, though, Ise has become even more of a draw because it has gained popularity as a power spot. In 2010, which was not a year in which new shrine buildings were completed, there were a record-breaking 8.6 million visitors. It is also notable that in 2011, the price of land in a commercial district close to the shrine showed the eighth sharpest increase in Japan, and was the only place in provincial Mie Prefecture where land value went up (Yomiuri Shimbun, September 21, 2011). When the shrine complex was rebuilt in 2013, a record number of 14,200,000 people came to visit.

One way in which information about power spots is disseminated is through books and magazines dedicated to them. These usually have the same format as regular travel guides, describing the history of a featured spot and providing information on accommodations, restaurants, and tourist attractions in the vicinity. The term *power spot* is neither religious nor weighted with tradition. The term is so well known that publishers can introduce sacred sites as tourist destinations and mention pilgrimages without making readers feel uncomfortable. Nowadays it would be difficult to find a Japanese guidebook that does not mention power spots.

Interestingly, the term *power spot* is a convenient one for public organizations, which normally must be scrupulous about the handling of religion. As was the case seen in chapter 4 with Aomori's pamphlets on power spots and mysterious regions, tourist bureaus and municipal governments throughout Japan are presenting local shrines, temples, and religious facilities as power spots. The official website of Hachiman City, Kyoto, for example, ran an article about a sightseeing activity in May 2013 called "A Visit to Power Spots at Iwashimizu Hachimangu Shrine." One of the photos on this website page was captioned, "Visitors touched the *torii* gate and Symbol Tower to feel their power." Needless to say, touching objects and absorbing their energy is not a traditional style of worship at shrines.

Amanohashidate, a sandbar in northern Kyoto Prefecture, is considered one of Japan's three great sights. The local tourist office has produced a power-spot map for visiting three shrines in the area. This map gives detailed descriptions of each shrine in traditional Shinto terms. In addition, it includes new statements such as, "Your love will come to fruition when you place a stone on the *torii* gate." The map refers to one of the shrines, Manai Shrine, as "Japan's oldest power spot, known only to the few." It also introduces the well in this shrine's precincts as a source of healing water.

In Shizuoka Prefecture, power-spot information is provided by the Shizuoka Geographic Information System (GIS) website. This website provides public information on city planning, earthquakes, and archaeological sites. In addition, the GIS has an entry titled "Angel Power Spots in the Mount Fuji region," which shows a map of power spots for finding love, marriage, and fertility, with a heavily subscribed comment section from website readers. The map identifies power spots at parks and beaches, as well as at numerous temples and shrines. Holding a wedding at Fujisan Hongu Sengen Shrine, says the map, will ensure a happy marriage. Kunozan Toshogu Shrine in Shizuoka City, the head of all the Toshogu shrines throughout Japan and home to a number of national treasures and nationally designated important cultural properties, is introduced as a place with a 1,159-step stairway that couples pursuing a romance may want to climb together, encouraging each other to get to the top.

Reinforced power spots

In the previous section we looked at holy places that may have already had long-held name value, but are now being renamed as power spots. The reinforced type of power spot discussed in this section is one that places new emphasis on elements not recognized before, such as the power to grant a certain type of prayer, or a particular part of the shrine or temple's precincts. This type appears to actively encourage its perception as a power spot.

A good example is the historic Hakone Shrine in Kanagawa Prefecture, south of Tokyo. Minamoto no Yoritomo, the founder of the Kamakura Shogunate (1185–1333), prayed here every New Year's Day, so it was long revered by samurai warriors. Today it is known for its *setsubun* festival, in which people celebrate the last day of winter by scattering beans to drive away devils. Although this is a common tradition throughout Japan, what makes this particular festival unique is that men wearing devil masks water-ski on the nearby lake.

Recently, another shrine on the Hakone Shrine grounds has been drawing attention as a power spot. This shrine, known as Kuzuryu Shrine, is a new branch of the original shrine of the same name that still stands on the shore of nearby Lake Ashinoko. It enshrines a dragon god, which is said to answer prayers for luck with money, good business, and matchmaking. Of all these benefits, matchmaking has been highlighted, resulting in a growing number of young female visitors. In 2010, Kuzuryu Shrine installed the "Dragon God Fountain" in front of its building, which draws water from a spring well. The shrine bottles and sells the water, claiming that it has healing and purifying properties. When you visit

Hakone Shrine and are purified by the priest, you are given a ticket that you can exchange for a bottle of this water.

Young women are often the target of the recent mass-media-fueled power-spot boom. Many power spots are reputed to work wonders when it comes to matchmaking and finding love. An example is Tokyo Daijingu Shrine in Iidabashi, Tokyo, a famous power spot for love and marriage. In 1900, Prince Harunomiya Yoshihito (later Emperor Taisho) made his marriage vows at the Imperial Palace altar. Tokyo Daijingu was the first to imitate this Shinto wedding style for ordinary couples. This has led to its fame as a power spot for matchmaking.

These days, many women visit the shrine, so it has taken measures to welcome them. For instance, it is the first shrine in Japan to install mist blowers for cooling off during the summer. Tokyo Daijingu also offers special goods, such as key-shaped charms (to open up the heart of one's love) and amulets to help one find a romantic relationship. There are also amulets printed with Hello Kitty or designed with characters from children's brand-name clothing. Since 2008, the shrine has been making

Tokyo Daijingu Shrine throngs with visitors, especially on weekends.

small wooden plaques on which each year's animal of the Chinese zodiac is drawn by Abe Hiroshi, a well-known author of picture books; these, too, are popular with female visitors.

Seimei Shrine in Kyoto (Plate 12) is another example of a "reinforced" power spot, though it is unrelated to the search for love. This shrine is dedicated to Abe no Seimei, a famous tenth-century yin-yang master. The shrine was built in 1007 on a large lot, but was later destroyed by war and left in disrepair until 1950 when it was finally refurbished. It began to draw worshipers from across the country in the 1990s, when various works of fiction based on the life of Abe no Seimei were released. Significant influences came from the novel *Onmyoji* (1988) by Yumemakura Baku, followed by a popular manga by Okano Reiko, television dramas, and movies. Abe no Seimei is a mysterious figure for whom few historical documents are available. Precisely for this reason, a series of fictions was created to foster the image of the *onmyoji* as a smart, cool, good-looking man. In movies and dramas, handsome actors played the role of Abe no

A visitor touching a holy tree at Seimei Shrine.

Seimei, which has made Seimei Shrine popular, especially among women. Recently, many female fans of figure skating also pay visits, thanks to Olympic skater Hanyu Yuzuru, who performed his version of Abe no Seimei to the soundtrack of the film *Onmyoji* at the Pyeong Chang Olympics in 2018, where he won the gold medal. The shrine displays an ema plaque with a prayer written by Hanyu and many fans purchase the same amulet that he bought there.

Discovered power spots

This section discusses nonreligious places presented as power spots. These are often natural sites with unusual or scenic features. As described earlier, traditional Japanese animism holds that gods reside in all living things. Japan also has sacred natural sites across the country, including several mountains. Mount Takao, Mount Tsukuba, and Mount Musashi Mitake are sometimes called power spots, but they have actually already been designated as sacred mountains in the Shinto and Buddhist religions and have shrines or temples on the mountain.

In the power-spot boom, however, people talk about nonreligious natural sites where they claim to derive energy from something or feel a sense of healing. For example, magazines and websites often have articles on Akiyoshi-do, Japan's largest karst cave, in Yamaguchi Prefecture, and Yakushima in Kagoshima Prefecture, an island famous for its giant ancient cedars. Both are designated as special natural monuments in Japan and Yakushima has had World Heritage status since 1993. The cave and cedars are several thousand years old, so people often talk about gaining power from the energy accumulated in them.

The Cape of Suzu at the far tip of the Noto Peninsula, nicknamed Sanctuary Cape, is a power spot whose potency would seem to have some basis in science: polar-front and subtropical jet streams meet in the skies above the cape, while warm and cold currents meet in the surrounding seas, a unique natural feature said to bring good fortune.

A similar pseudo-scientific power spot is the Bungui Pass at the boundary of Ina City and Oga Village in Nagano Prefecture. It is located on the Median Tectonic Line, Japan's longest fault system, and is known for a "zero magnetic field," where energy is said to be retained by two strata pushing against each other. The Ina Sightseeing Association website tells the story of a Chinese qigong master who discovered an energy spot in the pass, which apparently has the power to "make people happy." A survey on the website asks visitors questions such as, "Did you feel any changes to your body after going to the pass?" and records their answers. Every day, the Bungui Pass attracts several hundred people who sit down and inhale deeply as a gesture of taking in energy, and then fill containers with water from a pipe connected to a groundwater source. Traffic on the pass has become so congested recently that the municipal government has decided to limit vehicles to tourist shuttle buses.

There are also "discovered" power spots with no pseudo-scientific explanations given for their efficacy. One example is Kiyosu Park in Kiyosu, Aichi Prefecture. This park long had a statue of Oda Nobunaga, a powerful Japanese feudal lord in the late sixteenth century. Then in 2012, as part of a celebration to commemorate the anniversary of Kiyosu being awarded city status in 2005, a statue of Nobunaga's wife Nohime was relocated from Kiyosu Castle Square to stand beside her husband. The city's website calls the park a "place of commencement—hill of love and hope for couples" and introduces it as a power spot, where you can pray for a strong marital bond, successful marriage proposal, advancement in life, and unfailing victory. These "discovered" power spots are unrelated to any existing religion and many are government-endorsed.

We have so far discussed three types of power spots—renamed, reinforced, and discovered—between which the lines are rather fuzzy. A power spot that appears to be of the reinforced type, for example, may be regarded as a renamed type by locals. The tomb of Christ in the village of Shingo, discussed in chapter 4, generally falls into the discovered category, but for local people, it is actually a reinforced type. Accordingly, the three types are not for categorization, but only to provide clues to understanding the relationship between a place and the people associated with it, as well as their perception of it.

The consequences of the power-spot boom

The spread of the term *power spot* has made it possible for stakeholders to present religious ideas and practices as if they were not really related to religion, as shown by the examples given in the preceding section on the three types of power spots.

With the spread of the neutral-sounding term "power spot," people have started talking about "receiving energy or power" or "inviting happiness." These phrases have allowed them to express religious matters in public, without the need to use religious terms such as virtue or divine grace. Ordinary words are easier to accept for people with no particular faith because they are not associated with a religion or a sect.

Thus the circulation of new words and phrases has contributed to revitalizing existing holy places and giving birth to a number of new ones. In modern society, people can go on a pilgrimage while keeping their distance from traditional religion. What does all this mean for existing religions? We will look into two cases in Tokyo.

Kiyomasa's Well at Meiji Shrine

First let's look at Meiji Shrine, the epitome of a power spot. Founded in 1920, Meiji Shrine is dedicated to the deified spirits of Emperor Meiji and his wife, Empress Shoken. Located in the central Tokyo district of Shibuya, Meiji Shrine is one of the best known sacred places in Japan. During the first three days of every January, when it is customary for the Japanese to make shrine visits to pray for health and happiness in the

People praying at Kiyomasa's Well.

coming year, Meiji Shrine draws over three million people, more than any other shrine.

Inside the shrine precincts is the Imperial Garden with a spring well called Kiyomasa no ido, meaning Kiyomasa's Well. You have to pay an admission fee to enter the garden from an entrance that is separate from the shrine's main gate. In the 1500s this garden was the site of the home of feudal lord Kato Tadahiro, the son of Kato Kiyomasa, a famous military commander, who is rumored to have dug the well.

All of a sudden on December 24, 2009, Kiyomasa's Well, rather than the main shrine where visitors usually worship, was highlighted as a power spot. On this day, Shimada Shuhei, a media personality known for his palm reading, appeared on television and cited the well as a spot where people could invite good fortune. Although this was not the first time the well had been rumored to have special powers, Shimada turned it into a popular spot overnight. From the next day on, people started swarming to the well to pray for love or to escape from evil. At the height of its boom, people queued for four to five hours to get in. Today, it still draws many visitors, who take pictures of the well or wash their cell-phone straps or healing stones in the spring water.

To the disappointment of the Meiji Shrine authorities, however, many visitors to Kiyomasa's Well have been bypassing the main shrine. Meiji Shrine regards the well as a cultural property. This type of spring well is rarely seen in urban areas, and the official website introduces it as a place of interest, not a holy spot where you can expect to invite good luck or dispel evil spirits. The spring could never be an object of worship or faith in the eyes of the shrine. When people go to shrines described as power spots in magazines or on television, they often embrace sacred trees or hold their palms over objects as a gesture of receiving energy. Such behavior has no meaning to religious institutions. In other words, there is a gap between what institutions and visitors regard as the object of worship.

When the media designates a shrine or a temple as a power spot, the number of visitors increases, even though these visitors do not necessarily perform conventional religious practices. Naming a place a power spot sometimes adds a new dimension to its official story or established image. For this reason, not all such places feel positive about receiving so many power-spot seekers. In 2010 the *Jinja Shimpo*, a bulletin issued by the Association of Shinto Shrines, criticized the power-spot boom as a phenomenon of populism. The biggest complaint was that visitors pay no visits to the main shrine. An earlier article in the same journal had already broached this point. Visiting only the power-spot corners of shrines and failing to worship at the main altar runs counter to the spirit of faith, the article claimed.

Visitors are often seen heading straight to a particular spot, where they take up their positions—holding their hands over a tree, for example—and say prayers that have nothing to do with the deity of the shrine. In some cases, visitors only take photographs of a holy place, and don't even bother to make a gesture of prayer. Such behavior is born of the delusion created by the term *power spot*.

These articles reveal the frustration and resentment that shrine authorities feel toward the new myths or practices invented for their sacred sites. They fear that proper worship is made light of by television and magazines unrelated to the world of Shinto, and that people are being led to believe that new practices are more significant than traditional ones.

In Mutsu, Aomori Prefecture, is Osorezan Bodaiji Temple, one of Japan's holiest places. In this area of Japan, Osorezan is traditionally regarded as the home of the spirits of the dead. This temple, built on volcanic ground from which steam regularly erupts, is also famous for its unique scenery and its female spiritual mediums known as *itako*. These women gather at the temple during festival time and perform rituals tied to communication with the dead. The temple is often referred to as a strong power spot, but going against the tide, its deputy chief priest has said, "Osorezan is a meaningless, powerless spot" (Minami 2012). This reaction may be interpreted as criticism by a traditional religion of a fabricated image.

The power-spot phenomenon—the creation of a new image or myth of a place—may be interpreted as the emergence of a new religious authority. Holy sites managed by specific religions are invaded by publishers, television personalities, psychic mediums, spiritual advisers, fortune-tellers, and others who have little to do with traditional religious institutions. More often than not, these newcomers have closer ties to the general public, causing resentment among shrines and temples.

Imado Shrine

Earlier in this chapter we discussed the Bungui Pass. Unrelated to any particular shrine or temple, the pass has no traditional religion or practice to begin with, meaning that its recently created image causes no disputes. We have also seen that there are no disputes at Hakone Shrine, which has embraced the designation of its Kuzuryu Shrine as a power spot. Next, we will look at the case of Imado Shrine (Plate 11), which is actively enhancing its presence as a power spot and can be considered as falling into the "reinforced" category of power spots mentioned earlier in this chapter.

Imado Shrine is located about one kilometer (about half a mile) northeast of Sensoji Temple, one of the most famous tourist attractions in Tokyo and always bustling with sightseers. The shrine was founded in 1063 by samurai Minamoto no Yoriyoshi and his son Yoshiie as a branch of Iwashimizu Hachimangu Shrine in Kyoto, and was named Imado Hachiman. In 1937, it was merged with the nearby Hakusan Shrine and renamed Imado Shrine.

Standing by the *torii* gate of Imado Shrine are two signposts that say "The birthplace of *maneki-neko*" and "The place where Okita Soji died." The maneki-neko, a well-known cat figurine, originates with the story of an old woman who lived with a cat in Asakusa in the middle of the nineteenth century. She was reduced to poverty and had to give her beloved cat away. One night, the cat appeared in her dream and said, "If you make a doll that looks like me, it will bring you good luck." The woman made figurines of a cat beckoning with an upright paw and started selling them at the front approach to Sensoji Temple. They were an instant hit.

There are other temples that claim to be the home of the maneki-neko, but Imado Shrine's official website claims the honor for itself. The shrine makes amulets with a cat motif as well as ceramic figurines of a maneki-neko couple, which are both popular among visitors. Numerous maneki-neko items are displayed in a corner of the shrine office to reproduce the scene the wife of the chief priest saw in her dream one night. Among these are figurines from the Japanese anime *Natsume yujin-chou* (Natsume's book of friends), in which a cat plays an important role. They were donated when the makers of this anime visited the shrine to pray for a big hit. This display also attracts many fans of the anime to the shrine.

This shrine also commemorates Okita Soji, a principal member and one of the best swordsmen of Shinsengumi, a special police force established in 1863 to arrest or kill enemies of the shogunate. Okita suffered from lung disease and was hospitalized at the shrine, according to Shinsengumi records. These records include a memo that Okita died there in spite of treatment. Similarly to Abe no Seimei, the yin-yang master to whom Seimei Temple in Kyoto is dedicated, Okita is depicted as a handsome swordsman in novels, comics, and video games. Thus he has a broad appeal to young women, especially those who love history.

Until recently, Imado Shrine was known only to its parishioners. Its grounds are an average size for a shrine in Tokyo, but as it never had many visitors the decision was made to rent out part of the grounds for parking. Around 2008, however, women's magazines and travel journals began to feature Imado Shrine as a "sacred place for love" and a "matchmaking power spot." In response, the shrine started decorating its grounds with cat-shaped watering cans, park benches featuring famous animal characters, and flowerbeds with cat figures peeping out from between the leaves and flowers—not what you'd expect to see in shrines.

The grounds of Imado Shrine.

Today, Imado Shrine attracts many visitors, mostly women, even on weekdays. At New Years, there are queues of people who wait four to five hours to pray. This shrine is also written up in guidebooks published outside Japan, so busloads of tourists from China and Hong Kong have begun to make stops there. The current lively atmosphere was brought about by the shrine's strategy to go beyond their locality and appeal to a wider range of people.

When considering the shrine's power-spot strategy, we should pay attention to its focus on matchmaking. The shrine sells *ema* wooden plaques that are round rather than the usual rectangular shape. This allows for a play on words—the word for "round" in Japanese is *en*, which also means "romantic ties." In addition to these plaques, the shrine offers many other matchmaking-themed amulets and goods. The shrine deities Izanagi and Izanami are said to answer prayers for matchmaking, but they were moved to Imado from another shrine only in 1937. Now Imado Shrine has shifted its focus to these new deities as a way to meet visitors' expectations.

The shrine's relationship with the media is also important. We see that the shrine is actively giving out information, not simply waiting for interview requests. In addition to the official website, the chief priest's wife and his two sisters, the latter also priests at the shrine, have their own blogs. They have also published several books on matchmaking and power spots.

Another example of active media exposure is when a shrine takes steps to build a relationship with psychics who appear on television. The aforementioned celebrity fortune-teller Shimada Shuhei, as well as Ehara Hiroyuki, a self-proclaimed "spiritual counselor" who frequently appears on television, often receive negative reactions from traditional shrines and temples, but Imado Shrine is proactively making connections with them.

The priest's wife's blog describes visits by the celebrities to the shrine, and Ehara in return has mentioned Imado Shrine in books he has written. One of the priest's wife's blog posts is titled "Ehara Hiroyuki has done great deeds" and contains pictures of Ehara visiting the shrine on the day of the *setsubun* bean-scattering ceremony that marks the end of winter. The priest's wife gives Ehara and Shimada credit for teaching the general public about how they should worship at the shrine, as well as getting them to listen to religious doctrine, which she describes as "stories about the invisible world." This, she claims, is "extremely meaningful because of its purifying effect on Japan." Even her word choices seem to reflect the shrine's self-promotion as a power spot.

Are ties broken or created?

The example of Imado Shrine shows how a traditional religious site can adapt to the privatization of religion in modern society. People who visit power-spot shrines and temples do not accept existing systems of faith as they are. These people pick and choose from a variety of elements to make up their pet beliefs. This can give birth to new practices, such as holding hands over a sacred tree to receive power or rinsing cell-phone straps in spring water. These various elements are connected in diversified and creative ways, and this is one characteristic that sets power spots in modern times apart from celebrity gods in the Edo period.

As is the case with Meiji Shrine, the homemade beliefs and practices of visitors often perplex and annoy traditional religious institutions, which see belief in power spots as the destruction of tradition. Imado Shrine and Hakone Shrine, however, do not reject visitor's privatized beliefs and practices. Rather, they seem willing to take advantage of fads started, for example, by television psychics so as to expand the framework of traditional faith.

Not only Imado but other shrines and temples designated as power spots are often criticized for "commercializing holy places" or "selling holy things by the piece." The power-spot boom has certainly made it possible for many locations—from traditional shrines and temples to springs and mountain passes—to transform into this sort of commercialized holy place. These places are often presented as though they were merchandise in a catalog, with no attention paid to the religiousness or history unique to each place. People in turn choose and purchase whatever they like, hoping to receive the benefits and blessings they seek. This is one aspect of the power-spot boom.

The risk when a place of religious worship turns into a power spot is that it may lead to a breakdown of long-sustained ties between people and religion. Traditional shrines and temples have long-standing follow-ers whose cherished ties with the institution are based on family and local religion. In other words, religion has long been part of their daily lives and human relationships.

When the concepts behind the power-spot boom permeate society, individuals may become less likely to establish long-standing ties with re-ligion and come to see specific benefits and blessings as the only reason to participate in spiritual activity. For example, students may pray only right before an important examination, or travelers drop in at a sacred spot simply to kill time.

The opposite could also be true—new ties may be created because individuals relate to religion in more flexible ways. Since 2008, Imado Shrine has been holding matchmaking parties for single men and wom-en. These parties, once held only occasionally, have turned into a regular event because of the growing number of participants. The shrine takes applications and then chooses a group of hopeful singles by lottery. On top of that, shrine-sponsored matchmaking parties are unusual enough for Imado to receive quite a bit of media coverage on the activity. Thus, the matchmaking parties can be considered a device for enhancing the shrine's appeal as a power spot. The cycle of benefits continues as couples who meet at the parties and get married return to the shrine to offer their thanks. There are also many couples anxious to partake of the shrine's "power" who make a special visit there before getting married or hold weddings there even though they live far away.

Of course, these people account for only a small proportion of all the visitors to the shrine. However, we could say the shrine was able to cre-ate new ties thanks to the power-spot boom, which has opened it up to non-parishioners. The shrine has also made matchmaking into a product that offers specific benefits. It can certainly be said that Imado Shrine would have remained a local shrine with little relationship to people out-side the neighborhood if it had not decided to turn itself into a power spot.

In the twenty-first century, the power-spot boom began against the backdrop of an increasing diversity in religious tastes among individuals, and was fueled by the influence of an ever-expanding mass media that gives new meanings to sacred places. More and more people are visiting holy places as a result of the boom, but in the eyes of established religion they are nothing but nonbeliever pilgrims. The same is true for pilgrims on the Camino de Santiago and Shikoku pilgrimages. These sacred spots, however, are not merely places where people commercialize holy things and engage in material consumption. People may be seeking various experiences and exchanges in ways not prescribed in existing religious schemes, sometimes giving birth to a new type of "religious" community.

Looking at this from a broader perspective, the power-spot boom is indicative of the separation between belief and practice. The visitors to power spots are not experiencing the budding of a new religious faith. They are merely visiting these places since they are mentioned in guide-books and then act as they are expected to, praying at wells or writing prayers on ema plaques. There is no systematic belief behind their actions. They have simply been influenced by the media. Thus the power-spot boom can be understood as the spread of religion without belief.

Chapter 6 — Modern Society and Pilgrimages

This book has discussed how holy places—as distinct from other types of places—are established in society. Traditionally, holy places were thought to be managed by religion. A pilgrimage was defined as the act of believers who sought a rich experience of prayer at destinations whose holiness was beyond doubt. In those days, religious systems and institutions specified how a pilgrimage should be made and what it should mean. In a secularized society, however, holy places are defined based on nonreligious criteria.

This chapter takes a theoretical approach to sum up the discussions thus far. As indicated by the cases in each chapter, studies of modern pilgrimages require that we pay attention to people's sense of community and belonging to a group or a place. This is because a holy place relies on communal ties to make the place authentic. We will look at diversified ways in which sacred places exist today, by taking as an example the recent phenomenon of "anime pilgrimages."

The "temperature" of sacred sites

Let us roughly classify the many sacred sites we have mentioned in this book in the light of studies carried out by social anthropologist Erik Cohen and tourism and transport researcher Scott Cohen. The two scholars examined the process of and authority involved in the authentication of a place, and came up with two concepts—"cool authentication" and "hot authentication" (Cohen and Cohen 2012).

In cool authentication, socially recognized authority guarantees a place to be authentic, based mainly on academic studies and findings.

Typical examples are UNESCO's World Heritage sites and Japan's designated important cultural properties. In contrast, hot authentication means that a place is given value by groups or people with little authority or social recognition. In hot authentication, a place that looks fake to the objective eye acquires value through the activities of people with a strong attachment to it. In short, the value of a place is officially guaranteed in cool authentication whereas it is privately endowed in hot authentication.

Typical examples of sites with cool authentication are Mount Fuji, the sacred space of Sefa-Utaki in Okinawa, and Mont-Saint-Michel. These are widely known for their historic value and recognized by UNESCO as World Heritage sites. The Cathedral of Santiago de Compostela and places where the Virgin Mary has appeared are also cool sites because they are approved by the Roman Catholic Church, the world's largest religious organization. Whether secular or religious, the status and visibility of such sites increase when they are recognized by official third parties.

Cohen and Cohen discussed how cool authentication often turns places into something like museum exhibits. Look at Mount Fuji and the Kumano Kodo pilgrimage routes in the context of the World Heritage system. Their value is found only in faiths that no longer exist (Mount Fuji faith and the Kumano faith), and the self-awareness and healing experiences gained by modern-day climbers and pilgrims are unacknowledged. Another example is Shurijo Castle in Okinawa. Even though the original castle no longer exists, World Heritage designation of the castle site has made it an example of cool authentication. UNESCO's accreditation is widely accepted because it prioritizes the objective value of things.

The tomb of Christ discussed in chapter 4 is a typical example of a "hot" sacred site. It is nothing but a fake from the standpoint of history and archaeology, but today this place draws visitors because the locals strategically promoted tourism by creating the Christ Festival in the 1960s. In other words, the tomb has been given value by residents' continuous involvement with and strong sense of attachment to the site—these factors have indeed turned the tomb of Christ into a holy place.

A hot sacred site is often authenticated through interactions between locals and visitors. New sacred sites are emerging in long overlooked places or in places not considered as sacred, due to regional promotion, tourist development, and the mass media. Lacking historical or religious authenticity, such sites are made sacred by the emotional ties and activities of people associated with them.

The changed deities of Kanda Shrine

"Cool" and "hot" sacred sites are not fixed categories, and the temperature of a holy place can change along with changes in society. For instance, most holy places known for Marian apparitions turn from hot to cool sites. When a lay person claims to have seen the Virgin Mary, the rumor spreads and pilgrims are lured to the site. At this point, the authenticity of a miracle relies solely upon the witness, but later it will be scrutinized by the Catholic Church. The miracle site "cools down" when it is approved by religious authority and the witness designated as a saint.

As an interesting example of a cool site turned hot, let us look at Kanda Shrine in Tokyo, founded in 730 (Plate 3). It enshrines Taira no Masakado, a tenth-century samurai who rebelled against the Heian imperial government, was deified around 940 and was revered by warrior rulers in the centuries that followed. Shogun Tokugawa Ieyasu successfully prayed at this shrine for victory in the Battle of Sekigahara (1600), which led to him becoming the ruler of Japan, and Edo the seat of the shogunate. Kanda Shrine was also the home of a guardian god that was said to protect Edo Castle from demons. The shrine thus had a strong connection with the shogunate. The annual Kanda Festival, which still takes place today, used to be also called "Ruler's Festival," and festival floats were permitted to enter the castle. In the Edo period, Kanda Shrine was a "cool" holy place recognized by the government.

However, this shrine underwent great changes when the shogunate was overthrown in the Meiji Restoration of 1868 and rule was restored to Emperor Meiji. The Meiji government considered Taira no Masakado an enemy who had rebelled against imperial authority. Consequently, in 1874, his remains were removed from the main building of Kanda Shrine. A new deity was then moved in, Sukunahikona-no-mikoto, the god of crops, sake brewing, medicine, and hot springs. But even though the deities had changed, Kanda Shrine still had its "cool" authorization.

Masakado had been an enormously popular figure among Tokyo

residents, however, and they greatly resented his expulsion from the shrine that had long been an officially approved holy place revered by commoners since the days of Edo. As far as the local people were concerned, their own holy shrine had been violently dismantled by a new government comprised of officials from faraway feudal domains with no ties to Tokyo. The parishioners expelled the chief priest who had approved the removal of Masakado, and discontinued the Kanda Festival for ten years. They conducted a tenacious campaign to re-enshrine Masakado and their efforts came to fruition in 1984, 110 years after his removal. At this point, Kanda Shrine became a hot sacred site because of the actions and passion of local people. We should also take notice of media influence. In 1976, several years before his comeback as a shrine deity, Masakado appeared as the main protagonist in a drama entitled *Kaze to kumo to niji to* (Wind, clouds and rainbow), a popular historical saga broadcast on Japan's national public broadcaster. This is thought to be one of the reasons why the then chief priest of Kanda Shrine and the head of the parishioners negotiated the revival of the deity with the government. In this respect, the shrine can also be considered as a holy place created by the media.

The transformation of a cool sacred site into a hot one is noticeable in a modern society in which both privatization and information dissemination are factors. Kiyomasa's Well at Meiji Shrine, a spring in the nonreligious Imperial Garden, has become a hot sacred place because of information disseminated by the media. Its holiness is expressed not by Shinto practices but by the performance of visitors, who stand in line for hours to wash coins in the spring or take photos of the well, which they use as wallpaper on their cellphone screens.

The modern Camino de Santiago pilgrimage route is another example of a hot sacred site. The Cathedral of Santiago de Compostela, at the end of the pilgrimage, is a time-honored cool site where pilgrims can see the relics of Saint James, recognized by the Catholic Church. The relics, however, are not important to pilgrims who undertake the pilgrimage for nonreligious reasons. They walk the pilgrimage path seeking experiences of personal interchange. In other words, an act of walking that requires extra time and labor has made the pilgrimage route a hot sacred site. In this sense, we can say that today's Camino de Santiago pilgrimage is configured from two elements, a "cool" cathedral and a "hot" pilgrimage route.

Washinomiya Shrine and the spread of anime sacred sites

When looking at the development of hot sacred sites it is interesting to consider pilgrimages born of anime. Since the 2000s, the term *pilgrimage* has been used frequently to describe visits to places where anime stories are set. More precisely, this type of pilgrimage is defined as follows: avid anime fans find a place used as the setting of an anime story or related to its author, name it a sacred site, and then visit (go on a pilgrimage to) the place (Yamamura 2011).

Fans of novels, movies, and television dramas, as well as anime, have long been known to visit places where stories are set. For example, the Japanese public broadcaster, NHK, produces an annual period drama featuring a major historical figure. Municipal governments actively lobby the producer to shoot scenes in their cities because the resulting publicity almost always results in a huge increase in tourism. This well-known phenomenon, referred to as "content tourism," has been a major form of tourism in Japan since the beginning of the twenty-first century (Masubuchi 2010).

Today, local governments and tourist associations are mounting campaigns to attract anime producers, anticipating that this will spur tourism in the same manner as films and television dramas. Japan has several thousand sites that could be destinations for anime pilgrimages, for a variety of reasons—scenery used in the story, connections with protagonists or the author, the birthplace of a character, or even the address of the production company. Anime sacred sites also range widely from shrines and temples in the center of Tokyo to unremarkable spots in the suburbs, to famous sightseeing cities such as Kyoto and Kamakura, as well as the Shirakawa Go region in Gifu Prefecture, which is designated as a World Heritage site. The situation defies generalization.

Here let us look at a forerunner of the anime pilgrimage—Washinomiya Shrine in the unremarkable small city of Kuki, in the northeast of Saitama Prefecture, near Tokyo. Fans began to visit this shrine when the anime *Lucky Star* went on the air. Based on a four-panel comic strip by Yoshimizu Kagami, which was first serialized in a magazine in 2003, the story humorously portrays the uneventful lives of four high-school girls. In the anime adaptation, aired on television between April and September 2007, the main characters were changed to four shrine maidens at the fictional Takanomiya Shrine (modeled after Washinomiya Shrine). The anime used the historic buildings of Washinomiya Shrine and Ohtori Teahouse next to it as inspiration for the illustrations. Soon after the program began airing, a small number of enthusiasts discovered the connection with Washinomiya Shrine and went there to take pictures.

Soon the shrine began to be cited on websites and in anime magazines as the setting for the story, so it came to be known widely as a holy place for *Lucky Star* fans. A fanzine thoughtfully provided a map with directions. As the number of anime-fan visitors increased, the local chamber of commerce started holding anime-related events, at which fans volunteered to help out.

Statistics on visitors to the shrine at New Year (the time of year when shrines receives the most visits) show that in January 2007, before the broadcasting of the anime, 90,000 people visited the shrine. The next year, visitors more than tripled, reaching 300,000. The numbers continued to increase even after the series ended, reaching 470,000 in 2014 (Mainichi Shimbun 2014).

Fans visiting Washinomiya Shrine dressed up in shrine maiden costumes.

The Haji Festival and the *Lucky Star* portable shrine

The *Lucky Star* anime has provided Washinomiya Shrine with enormous name recognition. The shrine continues to draw crowds because many anime-related events are held there. Considering this, we can classify Washinomiya Shrine as a "reinforced" power spot. That is, reinforced with the anime's images and story, the shrine has extended its range of influence beyond its locality, presenting itself in diversified ways and attracting more and more people who previously had no interest in shrines.

But there is more to Washinomiya Shrine than this. The case can be analyzed from the viewpoint of community. The shrine is a sacred site for the fans, but they have created bonds with the locals that surpass the usual concept of sacred sites. Let's take a close look at the Haji Festival, which is held on the first Sunday of September every year. At present, two *mikoshi* portable shrines are carried through the streets in this festival. One is the traditional shrine constructed in 1789. Extremely large and heavy, this mikoshi is called the Sengan Mikoshi (*sengan* roughly means "three tons") and is carried around the town in the morning and evening of the festival day. In 2008, another mikoshi, based on the *Lucky Star* anime and painted with images of its characters, was created by locals and anime fans working together (Plate 17). It is carried only at night by bearers chosen from among fans, and it is carried behind the Sengan Mikoshi in the procession. When the two portable shrines reach the *torii* gate of Washinomiya Shrine, they are placed side by side (Plate 18).

The Sengan Mikoshi, the largest of its kind in the Kanto region, boasts a commanding appearance. It is hoisted by lively bearers in traditional *happi* coats. On the other hand, the *Lucky Star* mikoshi, much smaller and obviously made by amateurs, is carried by anime fans in their ordinary clothes. When juxtaposed, the two portable shrines seem to be at two extremes—one authentic and the other fake. They give an impression that an event made up by the media has been added to the traditional festival.

Tourism sociologist Sudo Hiroshi has pointed out that this element of fiction started invading Japan's touristic space in the 1980s, during the country's economic "bubble." During those years of prosperity, many regions lost their individuality and uniqueness as Japanese culture grew

The Sengan Mikoshi.

more connected and homogenized. To compensate for this, tourism began to rely on fiction to supply a sense that a place was special. However, in Sudo's argument, once the cultural climate of a place is lost, it is difficult to recover it with commercial strategies because a fiction spread to promote a sightseeing spot is unable to unite people or create a lasting sense of community (Sudo 2008).

From this viewpoint, one might criticize Washinomiya Shrine's transformation into an anime sacred spot as an act of selling local culture and tradition by the piece. In other words, critics might call the Sengan Mikoshi a symbol of the region's authentic culture and the *Lucky Star* mikoshi as something that has been made up, and that endangers the tradition. This anime sacred spot is nothing more than the outcome of strategic commercialization, and as such is unlikely to become a local symbol that citizens can empathize with.

Such criticism, however, does not apply to Washinomiya Shrine. In the first place, the procession of the Sengan Mikoshi began relatively recently. This mikoshi is so heavy that it requires at least two hundred people, taking turns, to carry it. The mikoshi used to be promenaded on bearers' shoulders during the traditional summer festival. In 1913, however, there were not enough volunteers and the mikoshi was set on a dolly instead.

Attempts to revive the tradition of physically carrying the mikoshi failed until 1983, when tourism began to rely more on what Sudo referred to as "fiction." In that year, a festival promotion committee was founded to call for shrine bearers from outside the city. Today, volunteers congregate from throughout the Kanto area, enough to carry the enormous mikoshi in the Haji Festival. These people are neither parishioners of Washinomiya Shrine nor members of a shrine support club (a group that financially supports the shrine). They are simply people who enjoy carrying portable shrines and head out to festivals in various places whenever they can.

More important, it should be noted that no deity dwells in the Sengan Mikoshi so there are no religious rituals performed for it during the festival. The mikoshi parades both ways through the commercial street leading to the main gate of the shrine, but never enters its grounds. The mikoshi makes no appearance in Washinomiya Shrine's annual grand festival either. It is carried only during the Haji Festival, which is sponsored by the Festival Promotion Committee, the local chamber of commerce, and a newspaper company.

Making connections with a place through anime

It should be emphasized here that neither the Sengan Mikoshi nor the *Lucky Star* mikoshi are merely tools to lure people to an event. Instead, these portable shrines suggest that a new community has been formed due to tourism.

The volunteers who come from outside the area to carry the Sengan Mikoshi may leave town as soon as the festival is over and may not come back the following year if they find a more convenient or attractive festival elsewhere. In this respect, carrying the Sengan Mikoshi is like a sport for nonresidents.

On the other hand, the *Lucky Star* mikoshi has brought about a bond among people who wish to support Washinomiya Shrine, even though their initial anime-inspired motivation for coming to the shrine may be considered superficial or commercial. These fans, who would never have visited the town otherwise, bear the mikoshi in the Haji Festival every year and visit the shrine on other occasions. In other words, *Lucky Star* fans feel a sense of belonging to the place. Thus the anime mikoshi is supported by a more sustainable community. Like the Sengan Mikoshi, the *Lucky Star* mikoshi does not enshrine a deity. However, the latter could be considered more "religious" because of the sense of community and belonging that it inspires.

According to tourism researcher Yamada Yoshihiro, fiction connects to the real world via bodily experiences. This creates a new type of tourism (Yamada 2013). His view seems true when we observe a hot sacred site born out of interactions between locals and visitors to Washinomiya. Many *Lucky Star* fans first found this shrine in a fictional world, but later came to carry the anime's mikoshi on their shoulders. This physical, tactile experience has given the place a new meaning.

The case of Jorinji Temple in Chichibu

Chichibu in Saitama Prefecture, about eighty kilometers (fifty miles) northwest of Tokyo, presents another interesting example of an anime superposing its image on the local cultural tradition. A pilgrimage around local temples began here in the fifteenth century. Later, in the Edo era (1603–1868), the pilgrimage gained popularity among the Edo populace because Chichibu was closer to Edo than the Ise Shrines or Shikoku. This pilgrimage route became known as the Chichibu Thirty-four Kannon Pilgrimage.

Jorinji Temple is one of these thirty-four, and its ordinary-looking building stands at the end of a quiet alley. This temple started teeming with visitors in 2011 when the television anime series *Ano hi mita hana no namae o bokutachi wa mada shiranai* (We still don't know the name of the flower we saw that day) was aired. The anime's opening scene depicted the Jorinji entrance.

This story portrayed the past and present lives of six childhood friends—three girls and three boys—in Chichibu, making use of the old-world atmosphere of this city surrounded by mountains. Scenes took place in Chichibu Station square, at Chichibu Bridge, and at Chichibu Shrine, and the city conducted a campaign to invite fans to go on an anime pilgrimage. Advertisement activities were also carried out by Seibu Railway, which runs railroad lines from Tokyo to Chichibu (Kawasaki 2012).

Muku, a local shrine, holds the Ryusei Festival in October every year, and the festival was also featured in the anime. During this festival, locals launch handmade rockets that look like dragons. Since 2011, this festival has included a tie-up with the anime, and voice actors from the program announce the launch of the rockets. Partly thanks to this tie-up, the festival regularly attracts an audience of one hundred thousand people.

Of course, not all anime holy places achieve harmony with local tradition or religious culture. As was the case with power spots, anime sacred spots sometimes emerge as the result of a great amount of information circulated through the Internet, and visitors to such sites have little or no contact with regional culture. In this respect, Washinomiya and Chichibu may be regarded as special cases.

Can there be a single-person religion?

As shown by anime pilgrimages, a modern holy place is sometimes created in a context unrelated to traditional religion. For example, a shrine in a residential area suddenly draws people simply because it appeared in an anime scene. An anime pilgrimage is an event that has less to do with traditional religion than a power spot.

This makes us wonder if "hot" sacred places unrelated to religion will continue to emerge in modern society, where values and world views are diversifying. The recent power-spot boom, in which media coverage of a "holy" place results in large numbers of visitors, would seem to suggest that the answer is yes.

Another question to consider is whether a single person's belief can turn a place into a sacred site. As we have already seen, a hot sacred site does not require the guarantee of a public system or organization. If this is the case, is it possible for a sole individual to establish a holy place through active involvement with it and promotion of it?

A place could theoretically be a holy place if even one person believes in its holiness. However, a holy place based on the belief of a single individual has no meaning in wider society and will not be passed down from generation to generation. To make a place holy, therefore, it must be given value by society. A holy site becomes meaningful to a society only when people talk and think about it as something sacred, and then visit it. In other words, people are indispensable for a place to be considered as a symbol of holiness. For this reason we are unlikely to see the unlimited proliferation of sacred sites.

When considering the role of society in the creation of a holy place, it is helpful to refer to studies made by French sociologist Danièle Hervieu-Léger. She is interested in the aftermath of the increasing privatization of religion. In modern times, individuals have established their own belief systems in accordance with their opinions and tastes. When this trend runs to extremes, will there be countless religions, each of which has only a single believer in the world?

To answer this question, Hervieu-Léger presented four ways for a belief to be accepted socially: institutional validation, communal validation, mutual validation, and self-validation.

Institutional validation and communal validation are equivalent to the validation of a faith by socially recognized organizations such as the Catholic Church or other religious groups. In other words, a doctrine should be endorsed by a religious organization of a certain size. In contrast, mutual validation has no connection to any established systems or organizations; a faith is validated by people who are bonded loosely together with similar thoughts. In this case, members join groups with relatively easy enrolment or interact with others with similar ideas in cyberspace, thus solidifying their faith. In self-validation, an individual intuitively feels sure of the righteousness of their own faith.

While presenting the four patterns, Hervieu-Léger immediately denies self-validation because it is backed only by subjective conviction. Such beliefs are unlikely to be accepted by others and unable to survive socially. These days, the privatization of society allows idiosyncratic beliefs to thrive. However, she argues, such beliefs cannot be sustained unless shared by someone else (Hervieu-Léger 1999). In other words, socially sustainable faiths are shared by systems, organizations, and other people.

Four patterns of sacred sites

Based on Hervieu-Léger's argument, we can classify sacred sites into four types depending on the type of supporting community: institutional sacred sites; communal sacred sites; event-based sacred sites; and personalized sacred sites.

Institutional sacred sites are established by a state religion, historically influential religion, or global organizations such as UNESCO. The value of these sites is rarely doubted in any society or cultural region. Examples are Jerusalem for Christians and Mecca for Muslims. In Japan, such sites would include the Ise Shrines, Mount Koya, Mount Hiei, and Mount Fuji. Other examples are the Atomic Bomb Memorial Dome in Hiroshima and the Arlington National Cemetery for the war dead in the United States.

Communal sacred sites are endorsed by specific social groups that are not as large as a nation. An example in Japan is the city of Tenri in Nara Prefecture, which is a holy place for the new religious group called Tenrikyo. Other examples are Mount Minobu, which is home to the head temple of the Nichiren sect of Buddhism, and the Honganji temples in Kyoto, which are the head temples of the Buddhist organization known as Jodo Shinshu. Examples outside Japan are the city of Sedona in the United States, and the town of Glastonbury in the United Kingdom, both of which are destinations for New Age tourists.

In relation to Hervieu-Léger's category of mutual validation, the author wishes to introduce the concept of event-based sacred sites, focusing on the limited sense of community and belonging. Here an event-based sacred place is defined as one supported by people who temporarily share a place. Many power spots and anime sacred sites would fall into this category.

As an example of an event-based sacred site, let's look at Burning Man, an annual summer event held in the western United States. During the period of a single week, several tens of thousands of people congregate in the midst of a desert in Nevada to erect an artificial city named Black Rock City. The event consists of art exhibits as well as workshops on music, theater, yoga, healing, and Zen meditation. A large wooden effigy called "the Man" is constructed at the center of the city as the symbol of the event, and it is burned down on the final night. Burning Man has its origin in the hippie culture of the 1960s. It is considered an event-based sacred site because of its fluidity of membership and the formation of an ephemeral community.

A Japanese example is the scramble crossing in Shibuya, Tokyo. This crossing bustles with pedestrians who come to welcome the New Year in at midnight on December 31. Crowds of soccer fans also gather at the crossing after big events such as a World Cup match. When the Japanese national team wins a game, fans walk across the crossing, doing high fives with each other. Japanese folklorist Takaku Mai calls this phenomenon an "urban festival." She differentiates it from traditional festivals because pedestrians only connect with each other momentarily, for example by exchanging high fives, and never see each other again (Takaku 2013).

Hervieu-Léger's final category, self-validation, makes a private sacred site possible—a place where one person feels holy, for instance, a family grave. Such a place is of course treasured by an individual but cannot have a wide social appeal.

The religiousness of connection

Hervieu-Léger believes that religiousness is based upon a sense of community or belonging. The gist of her argument is that it is not religious belief that binds people together; religious belief can only be established when shared by a certain group of people. In short, there is no religion without a community.

The privatization of modern society leads to the diversification of values and worldviews. Sociologist Suzuki Kensuke points to the scarcity of communal experience and the difficulty of forming a solid and permanent community in modern society. As a result, people find a sense of belonging in the fleeting excitement provided by a group, hoping to prove the *possibility* of connecting with others in a community. Now that communal experience is so rare, the mere possibility of forming ties, not a lasting relationship, can give individuals a sense of identity and belonging (Suzuki 2005).

Suzuki's argument can explain why the terms *sacred site* and *turning a place into a holy place* have been used frequently since the beginning of the twenty-first century. For example, the Koshien Baseball Stadium in Hyogo Prefecture has long been called the sacred ground for high-school baseball players. This is because players from schools representing all the prefectures in Japan gather there to play for the national championship. As mentioned earlier, the term *sacred site* has recently been used for anime pilgrimage spots. It also describes places that draw people with similar interests and tastes, such as venues for annual summer music concerts and other commercial events. Tokyo Big Site, a venue for a large-scale comic book market, is called a sacred site for comic fans. Another example is Akihabara in Tokyo, a district of electronics shops and establishments specializing in anime and manga. This district is referred to as a sacred spot for *otaku* (geeks). In reality, however, visitors to Akihabara are consumers of commercial goods.

As the segmentation of interests, tastes, and values becomes pervasive, just getting together with others has taken on a new importance. This may be why even the location for a gathering of people, such as Burning Man is metaphorically called a sacred site. Such spots are increasing to fill voids created by the decline of traditional communities.

Holy places with no gods

In a secularized society, the rise of modern "pilgrimages" has provided increasing opportunities for people to make contact with items or events that are "religious" in the broader sense of the word, but this trend is also leading to the weakening of traditional ways in which religion exists, particularly because of the ever-increasing number of event-based sacred sites. Sites like these essentially aim to attract as many people as possible, albeit temporarily, by accentuating elements of great appeal.

Folklorist Komatsu Kazuhiko sets forth an interesting argument about commercialized events as opposed to traditional religious festivals, using the classic Japanese folk concepts of *hare* (festival time) and *ke* (ordinary time). The term *ke* means day-to-day life of routines, whereas *hare* refers to out-of-the-ordinary festivity. In a traditional society, most of life was comprised of chores punctuated by a few celebratory events, such as weddings and regularly scheduled village festivals.

According to Komatsu, the balance of festival time and ordinary time has been upset. Our daily lives have become more eventful as society becomes more information-based and consumption-oriented. Komatsu calls modern society a *hare-hare* society, in which the boundary between *hare* and *ke* has become ambiguous. In other words, we get used to having festive experiences every day, which creates a growing demand for newer types of events with ever greater impact. Komatsu gives locally promoted "festival-like" events as examples. These certainly attract many people and create time and space different from the usual. However, Komatsu points out that such events "have no place for gods," which differentiates them from traditional Japanese festivals, which are usually religious in nature.

> [In Japan] A festival [*matsuri*] greatly differs from an event [*ibento*] in the worship of gods. A festival assures and enhances the relationship between god and believers, strengthening bonding among the believers. A festival is conducted for its devotees and everything is taken care of by them. No economic outcomes are anticipated . . . An event is much different in this respect. In an event, sponsors are aware of "customers," not "gods," and worry mostly about customers' responses (Komatsu 1997).

Komatsu argues that a religious festival functions to strengthen ties between believers, while commercial events are basically economic activities that cater to consumers. In other words, a festival creates a community, whereas an event simply spurs economic consumption.

This book has discussed the cases of Imado Shrine, the tomb of Christ, and Washinomiya Shrine, which now throng with visitors. But these places would have been forgotten if the local community hadn't undertaken activities to attract tourists. As a result of this quest for economic benefit, new and unconventional communities have sprung up. Walking along the pilgrimage paths of the Camino de Santiago and the Kumano Kodo, visitors interact with each other and with locals, and locals foster greater attachment to their community. These examples suggest the strengthening of ties between visitors and locals. However, such occurrences are not observed in all holy places. There are many so-called sacred sites that create only a transient community or regard visitors simply as consumers. These must be called godless sacred sites.

A new place for religion

It seems likely that "hot" sacred sites will continue to increase in the future, whether they are power spots or anime pilgrimage sites. Traditional pilgrimages, such as the Camino de Santiago or the Shikoku Pilgrimage, have become "hot" through the new popularity of walking pilgrimages. Modern sacred sites do not exist in places cut off from the outside world. Instead, they are created amid a flux of people.

Let us look at this phenomenon through the wider scope of modern religious theory. The burgeoning pilgrimage-fused-with-tourism trend is thought to accelerate the erosion of traditional religion due to secularization and privatization. One reason why studies on modern religion focus on pilgrimages is that diminishing church attendance and aging congregations make a sharp contrast with the many young pilgrims seen in holy places. In Japan, fewer people are practicing religion in daily life while more people have contact with religious items or events, for example, when they go on sightseeing trips to power spots.

An increasing contact with religion through sightseeing, however, is unlikely to revitalize religion in our daily life. Religion has reappeared on the public stage through links with tourism. However, tourism is a process of extracting impactful elements from religious culture or tradition, deliberately editing them, and spotlighting only the selected features. In other words, this process eliminates elements that are less impressive or unsuited to one-time consumption.

For example, let's say a tourist agency plans a two-night, three-day tour of power spots in Aomori and Akita prefectures. The tour has a spiritual theme, so its itinerary includes visits to shrines, museums, ruins, and sacred sites, including the tomb of Christ. We could say this tour is the epitome of tourism fused with privatized religion. Participants will visit interesting holy places and see historical relics, but such experiences will not get them to reconnect with their own local shrines and temples when they get home.

Nonbelieving pilgrims who visit modern holy places know little about traditional religions and practices, things that were once common knowledge. Such pilgrims will not gain knowledge about religion or its practice as long as they go on touristic pilgrimages. Thus the revitalization of pilgrimages through tourism is unlikely to bring about opportunities for people to connect with traditional religion.

The remembrance pilgrimage

This book is not simply a lament for the decline of religion; it presents the argument that the positioning of religion is changing in our society. A good example is the Tohoku Pilgrimage Project.

This project, which began in Japan during the aftermath of the 2011 earthquake off the Pacific coast of Tohoku, is carried out by volunteers from the prefectures devastated most by the earthquake and tsunami—Fukushima, Miyagi, Iwate, and Aomori. The objective is to console the souls of victims by selecting sites that were destroyed and mementoes of the damage and presenting them as a pilgrimage, so that memories of the disaster will be preserved. Candidate pilgrimage spots are solicited from the public. By 2014, eighty-nine spots had been tentatively selected and marked with signposts designed not to evoke the image of any religion.

As we have seen so far, a holy site is begotten when stories and memories of a place are shared in society. The Tohoku Pilgrimage Project aims to pass down the memories of the disaster to future generations by creating holy places. These include many shrines, temples, as well as statues of *inari* gods of harvest and *jizo* (guardian deities of travelers and children), which are deeply rooted in local life but unknown to the outside world. There are also some tiny street-corner shrines whose names are unknown even to locals. When struck by the tsunami, many large shrines and temples were used as emergency evacuation sites and have been linchpins for reconstruction activities. In this sense, places with a history of several hundred years have turned into symbols of recovery from earthquake, gaining recognition anew as "holy places."

The list of pilgrimage destinations also includes a lone pine tree that miraculously survived the flooding; Sendai Airport; a fishing boat driven ashore by the tsunami; an evacuation road in the city of Kamaishi; and a beachside shopping mall. None of these are religious but they have been chosen to keep stories of the earthquake in the public memory.

To outsiders with no knowledge of the disaster, the miracle pine is only a pine tree. But for locals who share the fearful memories of giant waves that washed away seventy thousand pine trees, it is precious. The lone pine died a few years after the earthquake, but it has been preserved at a cost of over ¥100,000,000 (about $800,000) as a holy relic of recovery. The tree shows how a holy place is created by people sharing a story. By connecting a memory to a place and sharing it as a holy site, it becomes possible to preserve that memory for a long time.

The Tohoku Pilgrimage Project is interesting as an effort to pass down memories using the traditional religious system of pilgrimage. The project is unrelated to any existing religious organization or tradition. Yet it can be understood as a religious effort to create sacred memory.

Changing the relationship between religion and society

In this book, we have studied how a space that looks quite ordinary to the objective eye can be transformed into a holy place in modern society. Traditionally, sacred sites have been controlled by religious systems such as the Roman Catholic Church and head temples of Buddhist sects. There have been systems for designating holy places and easily identifying pilgrims based upon a religion's doctrines and protocols.

However, in a secularized society, religious systems are losing their influence and power to control in the public domain, making the world flat. When society no longer shares traditional religious order or hierarchy, it is difficult for people to accept a certain place as being special.

Today, nonreligious entities such as media and individuals are at liberty to create a holy place by editing its story and image. As a result, people sometimes compare the religious site of the Ise Shrines with the nonreligious Bungui Pass using the same criteria, saying the latter provides greater benefits. In other words, what matters is the shared image of a place and experience expected to be had there, rather than the religious or historic value of the place.

These days, holy places are no longer supported by religions and doctrines alone. What is indispensable is a story that singles a holy site out from all the other places, as well as the bonding of people who share the story. Holy places emerge through ever-continuing interchanges between a place and its community of people. The rise of pilgrimages supported by such communities suggests that religiousness has shifted from traditional organizations, such as shrines, temples, and churches, to inter-personal ties.

In a secular society, religion no longer requires a "container" such as a church or a denomination. Religiousness is dissolving into the secular world. The rise of pilgrimages is an example of religion relating to society in a new way.

Afterword

The most challenging thing about writing this book was to discuss the relatively new theme of religion and tourism in a clear and coherent way.

The conclusion of this book is this: pilgrimages and tourism are becoming interwoven, with both being redefined and repositioned. These changes cannot fully be understood in the traditional framework of religious and tourism studies. My conclusion is simple, but such combinations and changes occur in various patterns, depending on region and religion. Verifying them individually enables us to gain insights into modern religion. The transformation of religion and tourism originates from the modernization of society; in the end, it affects our awareness of society and the way we experience the world around us.

This book covers a range of pilgrimage sites, many of which are connected to the Catholic Church, such as places where the Virgin Mary has appeared and the Cathedral of Santiago de Compostela in Spain. We have seen holy places designated as World Heritage sites; sacred sites born of the occult; so-called power spots; and sites sacred to anime lovers. The purpose was not to collect minuscule changes in modern religion to satisfy the interest of naturalistic curiosity. Rather, I was aware of the need to spotlight secular areas disregarded in the past. I thought religious researchers would find it valuable to consider how religion is changing amid the sweeping tide of modernization.

I have presented various cases from such a viewpoint, trying to make my writing as easy to understand as possible. Though not particularly pious myself, I went on pilgrimages where I walked, lodged, climbed up and down, and narrowly avoided disaster. I tried to base my discussion on actual experience and avoid academic jargon as much as possible. The readers are left to judge my efforts.

The writing was not easy due to various constraints, but it gave me an opportunity to reconsider discussions and concepts which I presumed to have understood yet had failed to pursue. For a humanities researcher, one's own past studies often arouse a sense of shame for countless reasons, such as reckless themes, endless fussy discussions, and the use of pedantic terms. To write this book, I reluctantly pulled out my past papers. Reconsidering them may have helped me sublimate my feeling of shame into better ideas.

This book would not have been possible without the instructions and support I have received from many people since I began my graduate research on pilgrimages. I wish to thank all and acknowledge those who gave me the guidance to complete this book.

First, Professor Yamanaka Hiroshi (University of Tsukuba) and Professor Hoshino Eiki (Taisho University) suggested that I take on the theme of religion and tourism, initiating me into pilgrimage research. The metaphor "standing on the shoulders of giants" means to discover truth by building on previous discoveries. I have not even reached the height of my professors' shoulders, but I would be delighted if this book could contribute something to the research field they pioneered.

I also wish to thank my schoolmates from the University of Tsukuba Graduate School for providing me with valuable materials and advice— Amada Akinori, Kawasaki Nozomi, Tinka Delakorda, and Toishiba Shiho. The four corrected my mistakes and helped me revise the text.

In August 2014, I was given the honor of presenting my research at the Graduate School of International Media, Communication, and Tourism Studies at Hokkaido University. As a result of this precious opportunity, I made numerous findings. I also established my own research policy thanks to the guidance given by professors Shimizu Ken'ichiro, Nishikawa Katsuyuki, Yamada Yoshihiro, and Yamamura Takayoshi.

Chapter 2 of this book discussed pilgrimages to Santiago de Compostela, which was the first destination I chose for my research. Santiago is an important place for me because I received advice and guidance for my doctoral dissertation from Professor Araya Shigehiko of Seikei University based on his own experiences there. He passed away in 2011, and I am sorry that I cannot show him this book. I later taught at Seikei University, and my teaching has inspired students to go on the Camino de Santiago pilgrimage themselves. I hope this little contribution is a way of returning the favor to Professor Araya. I am grateful to Otagiri Mari, Otsuki Miho, and Koga Eriko who spent their summer holidays on the Camino de Santiago and brought me back materials and the latest information about the pilgrimage.

Lastly, I would like to express my gratitude to my editor, Kambayashi Tatsuya. This project started when he read one of my publications and contacted me about it. This book would never have been completed without my trustworthy editor narrowing down my vague ideas into a specific table of contents, gathering materials, and reading my drafts again and again. Discovering his passion and personality through the process of writing this book was also a wonderful experience.

This book came to fruition thanks to the guidance and encouragement of my teachers, colleagues, and friends. I hope that it will reach as many readers as possible.

Okamoto Ryosuke

Bibliography

Allison, Anne. *Millennial Monsters: Japanese Toys and the Global Imagination*. Berkeley: University of California Press, 2006.

Amada, Akinori. "Honrai no matsuri no yukue: Wakayama-ken Shingu-shi "oto matsuri" ni kakawaru gensetsu no kyogo o megutte" [The future of authentic religious festivals: Regarding the competing statements of "oto festival" of Shingu, Wakayama Prefecture]. In *Kyodo saiko: Aratana kyodo kenkyu o mezashite* [Rethinking localness: Aiming for new studies on locality], edited by Hiroya Yoshitani. Tokyo: Kadokawa, 2012.

Beckford, J.A. *Social Theory and Religion*. Cambridge: Cambridge University Press, 2003.

Boers, Arthur P. *The Way is Made by Walking: A Pilgrimage Along the Camino de Santiago*. Downers Grove: InterVarsity, 2007.

Boorstin, Daniel J. *The Image: A Guide to Pseudo-events in America*. New York: Harper, 1961.

Catholic Bishops' Conference on Japan. *Statistics on the Catholic Church in Japan 2013, January–December*. Tokyo, 2014.

Coehlo, Paolo. *The Pilgrimage*. New York: Harper Collins (reprint edition), 2004.

Cohen, Erik. 1998. "A Phenomenology of Tourist Experiences." In *Nara University of Commerce Quarterly Review* 9 (1).

————, and Scott A. Cohen. 2012. Authentication; Hot and Cool. *Annals of Tourism Research* 39 (3).

Compri, Gaetano. *Seigaifu no otoko: Anata wa iesu kirisuto desuka?* [The man of the shroud: Are you Jesus Christ?]. Tokyo: Kodansha, 2007.

Dupront, Alphonse. *Du Sacré: Croisades et pèlerinages, images et langages* [Of the sacred: Crusadses and pilgrimages, images and languages]. Paris: Gallimard, 2005.

Eade, J., and M.J. Sallnow, eds. *Contesting The Sacred: The Anthropology of Christian Pilgrimage*. Urbana: University of Illinois Press, 2000.

Geary, Patrick J. *Living with the Dead in the Middle Ages*. Ithaca: Cornell University Press, 1994.

Graburn, Nelson. "Tourism: The Sacred Journey," V. Smith ed., *Hosts and Guests: The Anthropology of Tourism*. Oxford: Blackwell, 1977.

Hashimoto, Kazuya. *Kanko jinruigaku no senryaku: Bunka no urikata, urarekata* [Strategies of tourism anthropology: How to sell culture and how it is sold]. Kyoto: Sekaishisosha, 1999.

Hervieu-Léger, Danièle. *Le Pèlerin et le converti: La religion en mouvement* [The pilgrim and the convert: Religion on the move]. Paris: Flammarion, 1999.

Hoshino, Eiki. *Junrei: Sei to zoku no genshogaku* [Pilgrimage: The phenomenology of the sacred and the profane]. Tokyo: Kodansha, 1981.

————. *Shikoku henro no shukyogakuteki kenkyu* [Theological studies on the Shikoku pilgrimage]. Kyoto: Hozokan, 2001.

————, and Yashuhiro Asakawa. *Shikoku henro: Samazamana inori no sekai* [Shikoku pilgrimage: The various worlds of prayer]. Tokyo: Yoshikawa-kobunkan, 2011.

————, Hiroshi Yamanaka, and Ryosuke Okamoto, eds. *Seichi junrei tsurizumu* [Pilgrimage tourism]. Tokyo: Kobundo, 2012.

Ito, Masayuki. *Gendai shakai to supirichuariti* [Modern society and spirituality]. Hiroshima: Keisuisha, 2003.

Iwata Keiji. *Animizumu jidai* [The age of animism]. Kyoto: Hozokan, 1993.

Jinja Shimpo. "Ronsetsu: Pawa supotto—an'i na dento hakai wa tsutsushimu beki" [Education meeting: Power spot—avoid unheeded destruction of tradition] November 8, 2010 issue.

Jinja Shimpo. "Ronsetsu: Kyoka kaigi—kikai koryu no sokojikara shimeshitai" [Education meeting: Wishing to encourage the flourishing of our profession] November 22, 2010 issue.

Jippensha, Ikku. *Shank's Mare*. Tokyo, Tuttle Publishing, 2001.

Kadota, Takehisa. *Junrei tsurizumu no minzokushi: Shohi sareru shukyo keiken* [The ethnography of pilgrimages: How religious experiences are consumed]. Tokyo: Shinwasha, 2013.

Kawamorita, Eiji. *Nihon heburu shiika no kenkyu* [Study of Hebrew poems and songs in Japan]. Tokyo: Nihon Heburu Shiika Shuppan Iinkai, 1956.

Kawasaki, Nozomi. "Chichibu sanjuyon kasho, jorinji" [Jorin-ji, one of the thirty-four temples in Chichibu]. In *Seichi junrei tsurizumu* [Pilgrimage Tourism], edited by Eiki Hoshino, Hiroshi Yamanaka, and Ryosuke Okamoto. Tokyo: Kobundo, 2012.

Kimura, Katsuhiko. 2007. "Nagasaki ni okeru katorikku kyokai junrei to tsurizumu"[Catholic church pilgrimages and tourism in Nagasaki]. In *Nagasaki International University Review* 7.

Komatsu, Kazuhiko ed. *Matsuri to ibento* [Religious festivals and events]. Tokyo: Shogakukan, 1997.

Kosaka, Shunji. *Wabiremono* [The wabi-person]. Tokyo: Take Shobo, 2010.

Kume, Masafumi. *Itan no dendosha Sakai Katsutoki* [Sakai Katsutoki, the heretical missionary]. Tokyo: Gakken, 2012.

Lambert, Yves. 2004. "A turning point in Religious Evolution in Europe." In *Journal of Contemporary Religion* 19 (1).

Luckmann, Thomas. *The Invisible Religion: The Problem of Religion in Modern Society*. New York: Macmillan, 1967.

MacCannell, Dean. *The Tourist: A New Theory of the Leisure Class*. New York: Schocken, 1976.

MacLaine, Shirley. *The Camino: A Journey of the Spirit*. New York: Atria Books, 2001.

Masubuchi, Toshiyuki. *Monogatari o tabi suru hitobito: Kontentsu tsurizumu to wa nani ka* [People who travel in search of stories: What is contents tourism?]. Tokyo: Sairyusha, 2010.

Matsui, Keisuke. *Kanko senryaku toshite no shukyo: Nagasaki no kyokaigun to basho no shohinka* [Religion as a tourism strategy: The commercialization of Nagasaki churches and places]. Tsukuba: University of Tsukuba Press, 2013.

Michelin. *Michelin Green Guide Japan: Travel Guide.* Paris: Michelin, 2018.

Minami, Jikisai. *Osorezan: Shisha no iru basho* [Mount Osore: Where the dead are]. Tokyo: Shinchosha, 2012.

Miyata, Noboru. *Edo no hayarigami* [Celebrity gods of Edo]. Tokyo: Chikumashobo, 1993.

Nakano, Tsuyoshi. *Shukyo no fukken: Gurobarizeshon, karuto ronso, nashonarizumu* [The reinstatement of religion: Globalization, controversy over cults, and nationalism]. Tokyo: Tokyodo Shuppan, 2002.

Nakaya, Mitsuko. *Santiago junrei e iko! Aruite tanoshimu supein* [Let's go on a pilgrimage to Santiago! Enjoying Spain through walking]. Tokyo: Sairyusha, 2004.

Oda, Seitaro. "Sekai isan 'Kiisanchi no reijo to sankeido' sono sokuseki to kadai" [The history and tasks of the World Heritage site "Sacred Sites and Pilgrimage Routes in the Kii Mountain Range"]. Matsuyama: Ehime Center for Policy Research, 2010.

Odajima, Ayako. *Kizuki no tabi: Supein junrei no michi* [A journey of realization: The pilgrimage road in Spain]. Tokyo: Seiunsha, 2008.

Okamoto, Ryosuke. *Seichi to inori no shukyo shakaigaku: Junrei tsurizumu ga umidasu kyodosei* [The sociology of religion as seen in holy places and prayer: The birth of cooperativeness from pilgrimage tourism]. Kanagawa: Shunpusha, 2012.

Osawa, Masachi. *Zoho kyoko no jidai no hate* [The furthest reaches of a fabricated age]. Tokyo: Chikumashobo, 2009.

Picknett, Lynn, and Clive Prince. *Turin Shroud: In Whose Image? The Truth Behind the Centuries-Long Conspiracy of Silence.* New York: HarperCollins, 1994.

Saito, Sakae. *Iesu kirisuto no nazo* [The mystery of Jesus Christ]. Tokyo: Tokuma Shoten Publishing, 1974.

Seki, Kazutoshi. *Seibo no shutsugen: Kindai foku katorishizumu ko* [The Marian apparitions: Thoughts on modern folk Catholicism]. Tokyo: Japan Editors School, 1993.

Seki, Tetsuyuki. *Supein junreishi: Chi no hate no seichi o meguru* [The history of pilgrimages in Spain: Following the paths in "holy places at the world's end"]. Tokyo: Kodansha, 2006.

Singul, Francisco, ed. *Camino de Santiago*. Tokyo: Pia, 2008.

Sudo, Hiroshi. *Kankoka suru shakai: Kanko shakaigaku no riron to oyo* [The "tourism-ization" of society: Theory and application of tourism sociology]. Kyoto: Nakanishiya, 2008.

Suzuki, Kensuke. *Carnival ka suru shakai* [Turning society into a carnival]. Tokyo, Kodansha, 2005.

Takahashi, Katsuhiko. *Ryu no hitsugi* [The dragon's coffin]. Tokyo: Shodensha, 1989.

Takahashi, Norihito, Hotaka Tsukada, and Ryosuke Okamoto, eds. *Shukyo to shakai no furontia: Shukyo shakaigaku kara miru gendai nihon* [The frontier of religion and society: Modern Japan from the perspective of religious sociology]. Tokyo: Keiso Shobo, 2012.

Takaku, Mai. "Shibuya no shukusai: Sukuranburu kosaten ni tsudou hitobito" [The festivity of Shibuya: People who gather at the Shibuya scramble crossing]. In *Shibuya no kamigami* [The gods of Shibuya], edited by Ishii Kenji. Tokyo: Yuzankaku, 2013.

Terado, Junko. *Rurudo shobyosha junrei no sekai* [The world of the sick and wounded pilgrims going to Lourdes]. Tokyo: Chisen Shokan, 2006.

Toishiba, Shiho. "Hokkaido jingu" [Hokkaido Shrine]. In *Seichi junrei tsurizumu* [Pilgrimage tourism], edited by Eiki Hoshino, Hiroshi Yamanaka, and Ryosuke Okamoto. Tokyo: Kobundo, 2012.

Tomasi, Luigi. "Homo Viator: From Pilgrimage to Religious Tourism via the Journey." In *From Medieval Pilgrimage to Religious Tourism*, edited by William H. Swatos, Jr., and L. Tomasi, Westport, CT: Praeger, 2002.

Tsukada, Hotaka, and Toshihiro Omi. "Kokunai gendai nihon shukyo joho no hanran: Shin shukyo, pawa supotto, sogi, butsuzo ni kansuru joho bumu ni chumoku shite" [Information overload of religion in present day Japan: Focusing on the information boom on new religions, power spots, funerals, and Buddhist statues]. In *Gendai shukyo* [Contemporary religion], edited by the International Institute for the Study of Religions. Tokyo: Akiyama Shoten, 2011.

Turner, V. "The Center Out There: Pilgrim's Goal." In *History of Religions.* 12 (3), 1973.

———, and E. Turner. *Image and Pilgrimage in Christian Culture: Anthropological Perspectives.* New York: Columbia University Press, 1978.

Tylor, Edward. *Primitive Culture: Researches into the Development of Mythology, Philosophy, Religion, Art, and Custom Volume 1.* Cambridge: Cambridge Library Collection, 2010.

Umehara, Takeshi. *Mori no shiso ga jinrui o sukuu* [Forest-wise thinking will save humans]. Tokyo: Shogakukan, 1995.

Urry, John. *The Tourist Gaze: Leisure and Travel in Contemporary Societies.* London: Sage Publications, 1990.

Wilson, Bryan R. *Religion in Sociological Perspective.* Oxford: Oxford University Press, 1982.

Yamada, Itsuko, ed. *Shingo no minzoku: Aomori ken sannohe gun shingo mura* [The folklore of Shingo: Shingo village, Sannohe-gun, Aomori prefecture]. Hirosaki: Hirosaki University Faculty of Humanities, 2011.

Yamada, Yoshihiro. "Kakucho genjitsu no jidai no komyunikeshon to tsurizumu no aratana kanosei." [Communication and tourism in the age of augmented reality]. In *Advanced Tourism Studies No. 9.* Sapporo: Hokkaido University Center for Advanced Tourism Studies, 2013.

Yamamura, Takayoshi. *Anime, manga de chiikishinko: Machi no fan o umu kontentsu tsurizumu kaihatsuho* [Revitalizing the area through anime and manga: Contents tourism that makes fans of the town]. Tokyo: Tokyo Horei Publishing, 2011.

Yamanaka, Hiroshi, ed. *Shukyo to tsurizumu: Seinaru mono no henyo to jizoku* [Religion and tourism: The transfiguration and continuation of holy things]. Kyoto: Sekaishisosha, 2012.

———. "Nagasaki katorikku kyokai to tsurizumu" [Nagasaki Catholic church group and tourism]. *Tetsugaku shiso ronshu 33* [Philosophy and thoughts, Volume 33]. Tsukuba: Doctoral Program in Philosophy, Graduate School of Humanities and Social Sciences, University of Tsukuba, 2007.

———. "Shukyo to tsurizumu kotohajime" [Introduction on religion and tourism]. Grant-in aid for scientific research (B) 2006-2008, research result report "Basho o meguru shukyoteki shugo kioku to kanko bunka shigen ni kansuru shukyogakuteki kenkyu" [A theological study on place and collective memories on religion and tourism-based cultural resources]. 2009.

Yamane, Kiku. *Hikari wa toho yori* [The light comes from the east]. Tokyo: Nihon to Sekai sha, 1937.

Yinger, J. Milton. *The Scientific Study of Religion*. New York: Collier MacMillan, 1970.

PUBLIC DOCUMENTS AND REPORTS, BLOGS, MAGAZINES, NEWSPAPERS
Fujisan sekai bunka isan toroku suishin ryoken godo kaigi [Two prefectures conference on promoting Mount Fuji as a cultural World Heritage site]. "Fujisan suisensho genan" [Draft for Fujisan proposal]. 2011.

"Kirisuto wa nihon de shinda" [Jesus Christ Died in Japan], *Mainichi Graphic Weekly* magazine, 1973 December 23 issue.

Sekai isan o katsuyo shita kenko zoshin kanko no arikata ni kansuru kiso chosa chosa hokokusho [Basic survey of health promotion tourism at World Heritage sites]. Ministry of Land, Infrastructure, Transport and Tourism, and the Kinki District Transport Bureau, Wakayama Prefecture, March, 2005.

"Washinomiya jinja hatsumode kyaku yonen renzoku 47-man nin de junrei teichaku" [Pilgrimage to Washinomiya Shrine: draws 470,000 New Year's visitors for four consecutive years]. *Mainichi Shimbun*, January 24, 2014.

Yanagita, Kunio. "Seikokan aishi" [Sad Stories of Seikokan]. *Bungeishunju* magazine, 1926 September issue.

"Katte ni Tohoku sekai isan, No. 32: Kirisuto no haka" [Making a personal list of World Heritage sites of the Tohoku region, Number 32: Christ's tomb]. Takahashi, Daisuke and *Asahi Shimbun*, May 12, 2012.

ONLINE SOURCES

Decree according to which is granted a daily Plenary Indulgence on the 150th Anniversary of the Apparition of the Blessed Virgin Mary at Lourdes. Given in Rome, at the Offices of the Apostolic Penitentiary, 21 November 2007, on the Feast of the Presentation of the Blessed Virgin Mary. catholicnewsagency.com/lourdes08/indulgence.php

Sasakawa Sports Foundation "Gyosei to sonmin ittai to nari muraokoshi o" [Revitalizing the village with the municipality and the villagers]. ssf.or.jp/topics/tabid/1057/Default.aspx

WEBSITES

Agency for Cultural Affairs, Government of Japan bunka.go.jp
Aomori Prefectural Government pref.aomori.lg.jp
Catholic Bishops' Conference of Japan cbcj.catholic.jp/jpn
Council for promoting the Shikoku Pilgrimage route as a cultural World Heritage site 88sekaiisan.org/
CSA csa.eu
Ina Sightseeing Association website inashi-kankoukyoukai.jp
Imado Shrine members2.jcom.home.ne.jp/imadojinja/T1.htm
Kiyosu City city.kiyosu.aichi.jp/kiyosu_brand/power_spot.html
Medjugorje Place of Prayer and Reconciliation medjugorje.hr
Meiji Shrine meijijingu.or.jp
Nagasaki Pilgrimage Center nagasaki-junrei-center.jp
Shingo Village vill.shingo.aomori.jp
Shizuoka Geographic Information System gis.pref.shizuoka.jp/
Yawata City city.yawata.kyoto.jp/0000001142.html

About the Author

Okamoto Ryosuke

Born in Tokyo in 1979, Okamoto is an associate professor of Media and Communication Studies at Hokkaido University. He graduated from the College of Letters at Ritsumeikan University and completed his doctorate at the Graduate School of Humanities and Social Sciences, Tsukuba University. He specializes in religious studies and the sociology of tourism.

His published books in Japanese include *Seichi to inori no shukyo shakaigaku* (The sociology of religion as seen in holy places and prayer, 2012) which received the Japanese Association for Religious Studies Award for Outstanding Scholarship in 2013, and *Edo Tokyo no seichi wo aruku* (Visiting Tokyo's sacred sites from the Edo period, 2017). He has also coauthored *Seichi junrei tsurizumu* (Pilgrimage tourism, 2012), *Shukyo to shakai no furontia* (The frontier of religion and society, 2012), and *Higashi Ajia kankogaku* (Tourism studies in east Asia, 2017).

About the Translators

Deborah Iwabuchi is a US-born translator who lives in Gunma Prefecture. Her recent translations include Takagi Nobuko's *Translucent Tree* and a co-translation of Saito Hiroshi's *Rudolf and Ippai Attena*.

Enda Kazuko is a Japanese translator who lives in Tokyo. Her recent works include a writing textbook for Japanese called *Ultimate English Writing* and a co-translation of Saito Hiroshi's *Rudolf and Ippai Attena*.

＜英文版＞　聖地巡礼——世界遺産からアニメの舞台まで
Pilgrimages in the Secular Age: From El Camino to Anime

2019 年 3 月 27 日　第 1 刷発行

著　者　　岡本亮輔
訳　者　　岩渕デボラ、遠田和子
発行所　　一般財団法人　出版文化産業振興財団
　　　　　〒 101-0051　東京都千代田区神田神保町 3-12-3
　　　　　電話　03-5211-7282（代）
　　　　　ホームページ　http://www.jpic.or.jp/
印刷・製本所　大日本印刷株式会社